THE GREAT IRISH BOOK OF GAELIC GAMES

EVANNE NÍ CHUILINN

ILLUSTRATED BY
DONOUGH O'MALLEY

ABOUT THE AUTHOR

EVANNE is a sports presenter and journalist with RTÉ. During the (almost) two decades she's spent at the broadcaster, Evanne has worked on everything from World Cups to Olympic Games to All-Ireland finals, and she spent much of her early career dedicated to Gaelic games coverage. A proud Kilkenny Cat and Gaeilgeoir, she lives in Dublin with her husband, Brian, and three sports-mad children, Séimí, Peigí and Teidí.

ABOUT THE ILLUSTRATOR

DONOUGH is an illustrator from the 'world famous' town of Carrickmacross, Co. Monaghan. As a kid he was terrible at football, but was on an Ulster-championship-winning rounders team. In over twenty years' drawing, he has illustrated more than thirty books and countless other projects, and worked with people from Argentina to Australia and everywhere in between.

He currently lives in the English beach city of Brighton (which is nearly as famous as Carrickmacross) with his wife, Emily, and their slightly mad rescue dog, Esteban.

CONTENTS

Introduction 4

THE HISTORY

The History of Gaelic Games 8
The Gaelic Athletic Association 10
Where Are We Now? 12
Club and County 14
County Colours 16
Spotlight on: Michael Cusack 18

THE SMALL BALL

The Fastest Field Sport in the World 22
Camogie is Class 24
The Tools of the Game 26
Famous Hurling Teams 28
Giants of the Game 30
Legendary Hurling Managers 32
Poc Fada 34
GAA Handball 36
GAA Rounders 38
Spotlight on the King: Henry Sheflin 40

THE BIG BALL

Gaelic Football 44
Decades and Dynasties 46
Ladies' Football 48
Giants of the Game 50
Famous Football Rivalries 52
Brilliant Bainisteoirí 54
Aussie Rules 56
International Rules 58
Spotlight on: Rena Buckley 60

THE BIG MATCH DAY

Fields in Focus 64
Croke Park: The History 66
Croke Park: Behind the Scenes 68
Parades and Pageantry 70
Match Day 72
The Fans 74
The Lingo 76
The Media 78
The Silverware 80
Spotlight On: Mícheál Ó Muircheartaigh 82

CALLING ALL GAELS!

GAA around the World 86
An Ghaeilge agus an Cultúr 88
Cúl Kids 90

Acknowledgements 92
Index 93–95

INTRODUCTION

WHEN I DRIVE around Ireland, on the way to matches or to visit my family, I like to play a little game. How many GAA club pitches can I spot, and what are the names of those clubs? Kilmessan, Killimor, Kilgarvan … Have I heard of them? Are they a dual club, and have they any county stars I can think of? If I've never been to a town or village before, I like to see how long it takes me to spot the tall posts. And when I spot them, I can't help myself from saying, 'There it is – there's the pitch!'

Now, you're probably thinking that this author needs to get out more, but there's a reason I know I'll find a pitch in every town and win my little game. Gaelic games are part of the fabric of Ireland and have been for centuries. GAA clubs like your own lie at the heart of Irish communities, whether you live in Dublin City or Danesfort village. Maybe they're hurling only, or maybe they play all codes and even boast a rounders team. Maybe they punch above their weight with small numbers across two parishes, or maybe they're a 'super-club', with dozens of teams at every age grade.

No matter the history or the roll of honour, all Gaelic games clubs have one thing in common: they were all founded after 1884. Why? Because that's when Irish people began to revolt against British rule and organise Gaelic games with their own distinct set of rules. The Gaelic Athletic Association was founded in Hayes' Hotel in Thurles on 1 November 1884, and the GAA set in motion a plan for the growth of Gaelic games, Gaelic clubs and Gaelic competitions that continue to thrive today.

When we talk about Gaelic games being part of who we are, we don't mean just here in Ireland. The games have spread far and wide, and one-fifth of all GAA clubs are actually outside of Ireland! Next time you go on holidays – whether it's to Jersey, Jakarta or Jamaica – if you keep an eye out, I bet you'll find the same tall goalposts that I like to spot in my little car game when driving around Ireland.

Scór, Féile, Poc Fada – notice anything about the names of these popular competitions? Tá an Ghaeilge fite fuaite sa chultúr Gaelach! There is a strong link between our national games and our native tongue, and it goes right back to the late 1800s when Irish people wanted to protect everything to do with Irish life. I'm sure you recognise the phrase, 'Tá an-áthas orm an corn seo a ghlacadh …'

Speaking of trophies, lifting a trophy in Croke Park is the greatest honour in the game. It might be for your club, your county or even your school with Cumann na mBunscol. One of the best things about Gaelic games is that there is a place for everyone. Whether you're joining an academy to learn the skills of the game or trying out football for the first time on an adult social team, you really can play from the age of 3 to 83!

Your great-grandparents listened on the wireless, your grandparents watched the Sunday game on television, and now you can watch games on a tablet! What happens behind the scenes on a big match day to broadcast the games for us at home? Does the commentator say 'hurl' or 'hurley'? Did the ref blow the whistle for a shemozzle?

Whether you're curious about how to play GAA handball or want to debate who should be crowned a brilliant bainisteoir, I hope that this book will keep you reading and learning and debating ...

Bain sult as,

Evanne Ní Chuilinn

THE HISTORY

PEOPLE HAVE PLAYED Gaelic games in Ireland for centuries. There is a historical reference to a Gaelic football match happening as far back as 1308. (Incidentally, during this game, a spectator was charged with accidentally stabbing a player!) Although some British monarchs attempted to ban hurling and Gaelic football in Ireland, they all failed. In the 1527 Statutes of Galway, the playing of ball games against the walls of the town was forbidden. Could this have been the earliest known game of GAA handball?

The hurling matches of the eighteenth century were reported in the newspapers and described in songs and poetry, and that's when the games became more popular, both among the gentry and the general public. But the traditional games of the British Empire, like cricket, rugby, tennis and soccer, were more popular and more organised. The founding of the Gaelic Athletic Association in 1884 changed all that. Its establishment was part of a revival of Irish culture, along with other organisations founded to promote the Irish language and Irish literature.

THE HISTORY OF GAELIC GAMES

THERE IS A long history of Gaelic games in Ireland. Today we pack the stands and salute the all-stars, but where did it all begin?

FADÓ FADÓ

There are lots of ancient references to games like hurling and football being played in Ireland. The Tailteann Games (or Aonach Tailteann in Irish) took place every August during the feast of Lughnasa for nearly 4,000 years – until 1169 AD! The games were founded by King Lugh in honour of his foster mother, Tailtiú. For two weeks, Gaels would gather to honour the dead, make new laws and take part in sports and cultural events. The sports included jumping, running, throwing, boxing, wrestling, archery and even chariot racing.

During the 14th century, a game known as Caid was played in parts of Kerry. ('Caid' is an old Irish word for 'football', though everyone says 'liathróid' these days.) The ball was made from horse or ox hide and contained an animal bladder filled with air. Caid was played throughout the Middle Ages. The matches would often stop and start, with breaks in play to wrestle or fist fight!

The National Museum in Castlebar, Co. Mayo, has a collection of hurling balls that were found by people cutting turf in bogs around Ireland. The oldest ball is from 1192 AD, while the most recent one is from 1673 AD. Every century in between lays claim to at least one ball!

KING EDWARD'S BAN

In 1367, King Edward, who ruled over Britain and Ireland, banned Gaelic games and tried to get rid of the Irish language and culture too. Imagine if it was illegal to play a hurling match at school or against a rival GAA club at the weekend. Well, that's what it was like for the people of Ireland from 1367 until the 1800s – that's over 400 years!

Hurling became popular in the 17th and 18th centuries, but it was mostly played by landlords and the gentry. Ireland was ruled by Britain at the time, and when Gaelic games started to catch on, the ruling classes felt threatened. They didn't like this new-found sense of identity among Irish people. They feared that if Irish people kept engaging in Irish culture and sport, maybe they'd try to overthrow British rule! They reacted by enforcing British sports at the expense of Gaelic games.

This led to a lot of anger and bitterness among Irish people. The rules for English athletics also didn't suit Gaelic athletics, so Irish people knew they needed their own set of rules and competitions. Only then, in the late 1800s, did the GAA begin to take shape.

CÚ CHULAINN: THE ORIGINAL ALL-STAR

According to legend, the first ever hurler was a boy-hero named Cú Chulainn. But he wasn't always called that. He was first called Setanta, and was a young warrior known for his epic hurling skills. One day, a blacksmith called Culann watched Setanta in a hurling match. Culann was so impressed that he invited Setanta to a feast.

When Setanta arrived, Culann's hound had been left outside. The hound was a bloodthirsty beast and no one had ever got past him alive before. Setanta, armed with only a hurl and a sliotar, drove the ball straight into the hound's mouth, killing it instantly! Setanta then vowed to replace the hound and guard the castle in its place. From that day forward, he was called Cú Chulainn – 'the Hound of Culann'.

THE GAELIC ATHLETIC ASSOCIATION

ON 1 NOVEMBER 1884, a momentous meeting was held at Lizzy Hayes' Hotel in Thurles, Co. Tipperary. Those present decided to set up an official organisation to govern Gaelic games, and the GAA was born.

ROLL CALL

A man named Michael Cusack called the meeting and Maurice Davin chaired it. If you recognise those names, maybe it's because two of the stands in Croke Park are named after them! Also present were John Wyse Power, John McKay, J.K. Bracken, Joseph O'Ryan and Thomas St George McCarthy. These men are known as the founders of the GAA. Archbishop Thomas Croke became one of the first patrons of the new association, along with Charles Stewart Parnell and Michael Davitt.

DID YOU KNOW?

According to legend, 1 November (Samhain) was the day the Fianna's power died. The Fianna were a band of ancient Irish warriors who were led by Fionn Mac Cumhaill. The founders chose this date because they wanted it to symbolise the rebirth of these ancient Irish warriors.

READY, SET, GO!

The founders believed that British rule had eroded Irish culture and heritage, including Gaelic games. They worried that traditional Irish sports would disappear, and they didn't like the fact that organised sports were elitist. You weren't allowed to take part if you worked in a manual job – if you were a labourer, mechanic or small farmer, for example.

So, playing rules were formalised, and plans were made to protect Gaelic games and open them up to working people. Four games were included in the original 1884 charter: Gaelic football, hurling, handball and rounders. Just a few months later, the very first GAA clubs started to appear all over Ireland. What year was your club founded?

Over the next few years, the GAA took off. County boards were set up. New rules for hurling and Gaelic football were written down and published in the *United Irishman* newspaper. The first game of Gaelic football under the new rules was played in 1885 – in Kilkenny, of all places. By 1886, almost 600 clubs had joined. The first ever All-Ireland Championships took place the following year.

(IN)FAMOUS RULES

RULE 21

Brought in 13 years after the GAA was founded, Rule 21 prohibited members of the British security forces from becoming members or taking part in Gaelic games. The rule was dropped in 2001.

RULE 27

Created in 1905, this rule forbade members of the GAA from playing or even *watching* 'foreign' sports such as rugby, soccer, hockey and cricket. Imagine not being allowed to play hockey for your school or watch your favourite Premier League team! Rule 27 was commonly known as 'the Ban'. It was lifted in 1971.

RULE 42

This rule banned the playing of non-Gaelic games in all GAA facilities. In 2005, when Lansdowne Road (now the Aviva Stadium) was being upgraded, the rule was updated to temporarily allow international soccer and rugby teams to play at Croke Park.

WHERE ARE WE NOW?

1884 IS A LONG time ago, and these days there are more than half a million official members of Gaelic games clubs, in Ireland and around the world. But Gaelic games are overseen by a number of different organisations.

THE GAELIC ATHLETIC ASSOCIATION

The Gaelic Athletic Association is in charge of men's hurling and men's Gaelic football. They set the rules and make sure those rules are followed! Important decisions are made at an annual GAA congress. This is where new rules are written down and old ones are challenged. This is also where a new president is officially appointed. Every GAA president serves for three years.

THE CAMOGIE ASSOCIATION

In 1904, twenty years after the GAA was founded, the Camogie Association was set up for women. The first All-Ireland Camogie Championship was played in 1932. Ten counties took part, and Dublin took home the first All-Ireland title. The Camogie Association has a similar model to the GAA. They hold an annual congress, and the president of the association is decided following an election.

THE LADIES GAELIC FOOTBALL ASSOCIATION

The LGFA was set up in Hayes' Hotel in Thurles, just like the GAA! But it wasn't set up until 1974, almost 90 years later. The first senior inter-county championship was contested by just eight counties and was won by Tipperary. The LGFA has a director general and a president. There are clubs and county boards in every county, which are entirely separate to the GAA.

GAA HANDBALL

The Irish Handball Council was founded in 1924. That same year, another handball association was set up – one clearly wasn't enough! Well-known republicans Eoin O'Duffy and Ned Broy were devoted handball fans. In 1998, the associations came together to form one national organisation. GAA Handball now have offices and ball alleys behind Croke Park. The next time you visit the Cusack Stand, take a stroll around the back and you'll see their impressive building.

GAA ROUNDERS

GAA Rounders has a national Ard Comhairle of elected members, which looks after everything to do with rounders in Ireland. It consists of 7 people in total, including a president and a representative from each province. They promote the sport and host tournaments. They also train referees and assign them to games. A special committee organises all competitions, and it is their job to maintain fairness in games. There are more than 50 active rounders clubs in Ireland.

CLUB AND COUNTY

THE WORLD OF Gaelic games is vast. You *could* say it's like an enormous, friendly octopus, whose tentacles reach all the way from Two-Mile Borris to Timbuktu and back again!

CLUB VS COUNTY

There are dozens of clubs in every county of Ireland, and more than 2,200 around the world. You can play for your club or your county – and, if you're very lucky, you can play for both! Clubs compete against each other in leagues. The best players in a county get chosen for the county team, though most will still play with their club. Counties play each other in provincial and All-Ireland championships.

THE GOVERNANCE BIT

Your local GAA club is just one small piece of a gigantic puzzle. Every GAA club belongs to a county board. County board officials organise matches, make sure that everyone follows the rules and help clubs promote Gaelic games in their communities. Every province in Ireland also has a provincial council. So, if your club wins the county title, your journey doesn't end there! Has your club ever reached a Leinster or an Ulster final? Only the very best then go on to challenge for an All-Ireland club title – the greatest honour in the club game.

DID YOU KNOW?

Lucan Sarsfields GAA Club is one of the oldest and biggest clubs in the world. It was set up in 1886!

WHERE WE ALL BELONG

Community and club are at the heart of the GAA. In fact, many famous hurlers and footballers say that the club game is closer to their hearts than the more glamorous inter-county game. Why? Because you start and finish your playing career with your club. What age did you join your local Gaelic Games Academy? If you're lucky enough to play for, let's say, Galway, I bet Oranmore or St Thomas' would welcome you back to play for them at the end of your career. Your GAA club is a special place, and a place where you will always belong.

A name that dates back to the 1800s, when most of the onions sold in Leinster were grown in Carlow!

Because of their distinctive all-white kit.

Because of their county colours – not because they're scaredy-cats!

ARE YOU A REBEL OR A YELLOWBELLY?

Some county teams have brilliant nicknames. How many of these did you know?

ANTRIM
The Saffrons

CARLOW
The Scallion Eaters

CAVAN
The Breffni County

CLARE
The Banner

CORK
The Rebels

DUBLIN
The Jackeens

GALWAY
The Tribesmen/Tribeswomen

KERRY
The Kingdom

KILDARE
The Lilywhites

KILKENNY
The Cats

LIMERICK
The Treaty County

MEATH
The Royals

OFFALY
The Faithful

TIPPERARY
The Premier

WATERFORD
The Déise

WEXFORD
The Yellowbellies

COUNTY COLOURS

EVERY COUNTY HAS a unique colour or colours. Some people think the Carlow flag looks like a fruit pastille lollipop – or better yet, a Rastafarian flag! Kildare is the only county with just one colour on their flag: white. Imagine how hard it is to get the grass stains out?

LEINSTER

CARLOW

LONGFORD

DUBLIN

LOUTH

WEXFORD

KILDARE

MEATH

WICKLOW

KILKENNY

WESTMEATH

LAOIS

OFFALY

Lots of clubs and counties used to play in green, white and gold. Then a special competition was held, and Offaly won the right to wear the national colours for evermore!

DID YOU KNOW?

The most popular colour combination is blue and gold, with no fewer than FIVE counties sharing those colours. Historians believe the combination became popular after blue and gold banners and flags were carried by Brian Ború in the Battle of Clontarf in 1014.

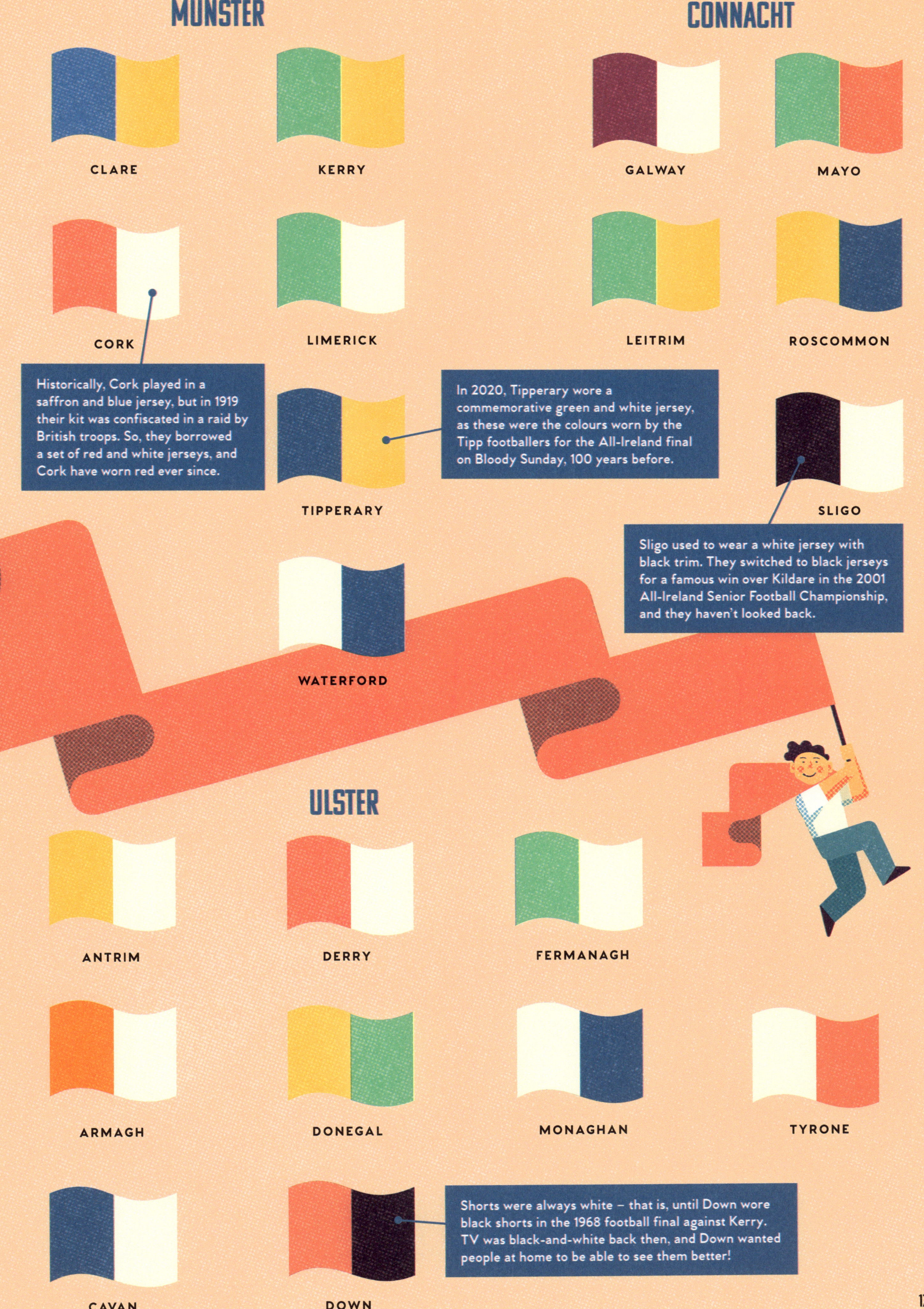

SPOTLIGHT ON: MICHAEL CUSACK

ONE OF THE seven founding members of the GAA, Michael Cusack was the man who called a meeting on 1 November 1884 to set up what became known as the Gaelic Athletic Association.

Michael was born on 20 September 1847 – during the Great Famine. His family lived in a small thatched cottage in Carron, Co. Clare. He had four brothers and one sister. His parents, Matthew and Bridget, were native Irish speakers. As a child, Michael only spoke Irish with his parents and siblings. It's said that he didn't use English or see an English dictionary until the age of 11!

The Cusacks were hurling people. Michael was a great athlete: he played hurling, football and cricket, took part in the high-jump and weight-throwing events and was a shot-putt champion! But even from a young age he could see that the rules governing athletics in Ireland were only suitable for Britain. The Protestant establishment did not approve of playing on a Sunday – but for a lot of people, Sunday was their only day off and the only time they could play. That's when Michael and his friends played hurling – on Sundays after mass!

Michael trained to be a schoolteacher. In 1876, he married Margaret Woods, and they went on to have seven children. Bit by bit, Michael got involved in journalism and politics. He had strong views on preserving the Irish language and culture. He was a republican and a member of the Society for the Preservation of the Irish Language and later the Gaelic League.

He could see that British rule was eroding Irish culture and traditional Irish sports, so he set about gathering a group of like-minded Gaels to hatch a plan!

Michael had a friend called Pat Nally. Pat was an athlete and a leading nationalist, and was just as passionate about Gaelic games as Michael. One day, the pair were walking through the Phoenix Park and noticed that only a handful of people were playing sports. They turned to each other: it was time to do something. Together, they organised National Athletic Sports meetings in 1879 and 1880, and that was the beginning of a movement that led to the foundation of the GAA four years later. Both Pat Nally and Michael Cusack have stands in Croke Park named after them today.

Michael had a big personality and was very good at inspiring people. He was also quite a character. He had a big bushy beard, wore a long coat and broad-brimmed hat, and liked to carry a blackthorn stick. He must have been hard to miss! He died in 1906, at the age of 59, and is buried in Glasnevin Cemetery in Dublin.

HURLING IS AFFECTIONATELY known to Gaels as 'the small ball'. The sport has evolved over many years and is among the most popular sports in Ireland, alongside Gaelic football. The rules for modern hurling were first set out in 1884 with the establishment of the Gaelic Athletic Association by Michael Cusack.

The Liam MacCarthy Cup is awarded to the best men's hurling team in Ireland when they win the senior All-Ireland hurling final. Camogie is the women's version of hurling, but it is a virtually identical sport. Teams across Ireland compete for the O'Duffy Cup, which is awarded to the winners of the All-Ireland Senior Camogie Championship. The small ball – or sliotar – is also used to play rounders (the only mixed-team sport in Gaelic games). The game of handball uses a smaller 'small ball'!

Today, hurling, camogie, handball and rounders are played around the globe, and some even have major championships across Asia, Europe and America.

THE FASTEST FIELD SPORT IN THE WORLD

HURLING IS THOUGHT to be the oldest and the fastest field sport in the whole world! Historians believe it may even have been invented as a way to train ancient warriors for battle. It is a stick-and-ball game that is played all over the world. The men's version is called hurling and the women's version is called camogie.

WHAT IS HURLING?

A definition will never do the game justice, but let's try! Hurling is played using a hurl (or hurley) and a ball called a sliotar. Teams of 15 players face off against each other, and the aim of the game is to score as many goals and points as possible in the time allowed. A goal is worth three points, and a point is scored when the ball goes *over* the goalpost but *between* the uprights. Hurling goals resemble the capital letter H, and the uprights are the two posts that rise above the goalmouth. Players must wear helmets for safety, though this only became mandatory in 2010. Each year, the Liam MacCarthy Cup is awarded to the All-Ireland hurling champions.

BETWEEN THE POSTS

The real heroes in hurling are the goalkeepers. Imagine facing down a penalty: you're standing in the goal with just your hurl for company as the ball speeds towards you from only 13 metres away! A GAA official once said that 'A key requirement to be a goalkeeper in hurling is that you have to be mad'. In 2007, the famous Clare goalkeeper Davy Fitzgerald lost a piece of his ring finger during a match. He had the finger reattached and said, 'I'm going back hurling hopefully at the end of this month ... even though the doctors think that I am mad to do so.'

DID YOU KNOW?

A lacrosse ball in play averages 120 km per hour, while an ice hockey puck can reach speeds of 160 km per hour. But the sliotar? In a senior inter-county game, a sliotar can travel at an average speed of 180 km per hour. That's faster than a hurricane!

READY, LOCK, STRIKE

JAB LIFT

The jab lift is usually done on the run, and it is the quickest way to get the ball into your hand from the ground. Crouch down, with the toe of the hurley pointing away from the body on your dominant side. Your thumbs should be pointing towards the bas, as you slide the hurl under the sliotar to lift it. Release your non-dominant hand to catch the sliotar, and away you go! If you're brave enough to be your team's penalty taker, you'd jab-lift the ball before firing it to the back of the net.

SOLO

You'll use a solo to move the ball towards the goal or away from the opposition! Hold your hurl out in front of you, with the bas flat and the toe pointing away from your body on the dominant side. Balance or hop the sliotar on the bas, and start running! For better control, hold the hurl halfway down with the non-dominant hand or use a shortened grip.

STRIKE FROM THE HAND

This is the best way to pass the ball a good distance. It's also used for puck-outs. Keeping your eye on the sliotar, toss it in front of you at shoulder height from your non-dominant hand. Slide that hand down to meet your dominant hand at the top of the hurl, and swing to strike the ball mid-air in front of you at knee height. Always practise this skill on your weak side too!

HIGH FIELDING

The best way to win a 50/50 ball is to jump off the ground and catch the ball mid-air. This skill requires bravery and agility. Step off the ground with your eyes on the ball and reach up with your non-dominant hand to catch the ball. Always protect your catching hand with the hurl.

HURLING 7S

Another version of hurling and camogie is called 7s. Why? You've guessed it: there are only 7 players on a team instead of 15. You need to be super-fit to play 7s hurling or camogie, because with so few players on the pitch, everyone has to work a lot harder.

There is a famous 7s tournament hosted every year by Dublin club Kilmacud Crokes on the day before the All-Ireland hurling final. It's called the All-Ireland 7s and attracts teams from all over the country.

CAMOGIE IS CLASS

CAMOGIE IS THE name given to the women's version of hurling. It is fast and furious and is played by 100,000 women worldwide.

BLAZING A TRAIL

Camogie was not included in the GAA charter of 1884. Nobody knows why for sure, but it was probably because of the role of women in society at that time: no one thought that women would or should play. Women wrote to the GAA to ask why they had been excluded. Some asked if they could at least play a role washing and decorating the men's jerseys. In the late 1800s, women's demands for independence and equal rights started to gain ground. In 1903, the game of camogie was officially recognised, and a year later the Camogie Association was set up. About time!

THROWING OUT THE RULEBOOK

The rules of camogie are very similar to those of hurling, although until 1999, women's teams had only 12 players versus the men's 15. Nowadays, camogie teams are also made up of 15 players. Just like hurling, the game is played with a hurl and a sliotar, and players must wear a helmet. Matches last 60 minutes and the players switch the direction of play at half-time. A goal is worth three points, and a point is scored when the ball goes *over* the goalpost but *between* the uprights!

DID YOU KNOW?

A second crossbar, or a 'points bar', was originally used in camogie. A point would not be allowed if the sliotar travelled over this bar. Imagine punishing a player for being so strong that they sent the ball too high! This rule was abolished in 1979.

WHAT'S IN A NAME?

The stick used in hurling was originally called a *camán*. Women used slightly shorter sticks, which became known as *camóg*s. The word was anglicised and that is how the sport got its name: camogie! It must have been very difficult to play in long skirts, but that's what early camogie players wore, along with canvas boots, long black stockings, a blouse and a sash around the waist or the collar.

Most early camogie matches involved 'ground hurling'. This means striking the ball on the ground as opposed to rising the ball and striking it out of the hand. Nearly all the scores were goals taken from placed balls. It was a very different type of game to today's fast-paced, physical battles!

CAMOGIE VS HURLING

While the rules of camogie and hurling are very similar, there are a few differences between the two. How many of these did you know?

CAMOGIE	HURLING
Goalkeeper can wear the same jersey as teammates	Goalkeeper must wear a different jersey
45-yard free awarded	65-yard free awarded
Can handpass any score from play	Handpass goal forbidden
Dropping the stick to handpass is permitted	Can't drop the stick to handpass
60-minute game	70-minute game
Size 4 sliotar	Size 5 sliotar
After a score, 13-metre puck-out	Puck-out from the end line
Metal band on the bas must be covered	Not necessary to cover band on the bas
Side-to-side charges forbidden	Side-to-side charges permitted

THE TOOLS OF THE GAME

EVERY HURLING AND camogie player needs two things: a hurley and a sliotar. These are the essential tools of the game!

THE PARTS OF A HURL

Do you call it a hurl or a hurley? This question often causes fierce debates ... Ask your friends what they call it and see how cross they get if you disagree! Here are the different parts of a hurley.

HANDLE: There is a small lip at the top of the handle, which stops the hurley slipping from your hand.

TOE: The toe is used in the roll lift or jab lift. These allow you to get the ball from the ground into your hand.

BAS: The bas is used to strike the ball.

HEEL: The heel is used to give height to a ball struck on the ground.

WHAT'S A HURL MADE OF?

Hurls are traditionally made from ash trees, because ash is strong and flexible. If you imagine a large tree trunk, the bottom part near the roots would become the 'bas'. Hurley makers produce all different sized hurleys from the same tree. Around 400,000 hurls are made in Ireland every year, but ash supplies are running out due to an infection called ash dieback disease – and so hurley makers have been forced to think of new ways to meet the demand. Nowadays, there are hurls made from both ash and bamboo, and there are even some synthetically made hurls. The synthetic hurls often drive the ball further but can be more difficult to keep control of the sliotar with, so they take lots of getting used to.

WHAT'S IN A SLIOTAR?

Sliotars come in lots of different sizes, but they are all made the same way. A compact sphere of cork is covered by two pieces of leather stitched tightly together. The stitching is known as the rib or the rim, and there are very strict rules about how thick or thin it can be. In the past, sliotars were made from all sorts of wacky materials, from hollow bronze and leather to wood, rope and animal hair!

DID YOU KNOW?

A wall ball is a special type of sliotar used in a ball alley. It's made of rubber and can be used in all weather conditions. Sliotars made of cork often become very heavy if they've been left out in the rain for too long!

SPEAKING WITH AN EXPERT

Seán Torpey is a hurley maker from Co. Clare. He makes 30,000 to 40,000 hurls every year! Seán gets most of his ash from the Netherlands, but a small amount also comes from Croatia and even Canada. Seán also uses bamboo. In fact, his favourite hurley is his Torpey Bambú hurley, because it's a high-performance hurley for all players, from kids all the way up to adults.

THE PARTS OF A SLIOTAR

There are some rules that *must* be followed if a sliotar is to be approved by the GAA. This is what each sliotar must have.

- Weight must be between 110g and 120g.
- Diameter, not including the rib (rim), must be between 69mm and 72mm.
- Leather cover thickness must be between 1.8mm and 2.7mm, laminated with a coating no greater than 0.15mm.
- Rim height must be between 2.0mm and 2.8mm. Rim width must be between 3.6mm and 5.4mm.

FAMOUS HURLING TEAMS

HURLING IS A team sport first and foremost, and while there are superstars in every era, no team can win with just one giant of the game on their side. Over the last hundred years, almost every hurling stronghold has experienced a golden era at one stage or another. No team can dominate forever, but there have been some very famous purple patches!

100 YEARS OF ALL-IRELAND GLORY

LIMERICK 1933–36
Limerick played in all four All-Ireland finals from 1933–36 and won in '34 and '36.

TIPPERARY 1949–52
Tipperary had a great team in the 1940s, but fell short in the Munster championships against the mighty Cork. There were no qualifiers back then, so there was no way to get to an All-Ireland without winning your province. Tipp ruined Cork's dreams of five in a row in 1945, but the real breakthrough came in 1949, and they went on to win three in a row.

WEXFORD 1954–57
This Wexford team is best known for the Rackard brothers: Nicky, Billy and Bobby. The 1950s were a golden era for hurling and showcased keenly contested matches, but they are remembered as Wexford's period of dominance. The 'model county' won All-Irelands in 1955 and '56 and were the first team to consistently challenge the 'Big Three' – Cork, Kilkenny and Tipperary – during that time.

KILKENNY 1968–75
The Cats won All-Irelands in 1969, '72, '74 and '75. The only 80-minute final ever played was in 1972. Kilkenny were eight points down and staged a remarkable comeback to beat Cork by seven!

CORK 1941–47
This Cork team achieved the first ever four in a row, winning the All-Ireland in 1941, '42, '43 and '44. It is also remembered for the fantastic players it boasted. Christy Ring was universally accepted as the greatest player ever (until Henry Shefflin's unrivalled reign as king came along in the 2000s). Tipperary stopped the five in a row in 1945, but Cork won again in '46.

CORK 1952–54
Cork won three in a row in 1952–54. In 1954, Christy Ring became the first player to win eight All-Irelands as a member of the starting team. A record crowd of 85,000 packed into Croke Park for that final!

TIPPERARY 1960–71
Tipp enjoyed almost a decade of dominance around this time. They beat Cork in a Munster final in 1960 for the first time in nine years and contested eight All-Ireland finals between 1960 and 1971. Jimmy Doyle was the hero of the day, but his final game in 1971 was the beginning of an 18-year famine of All-Ireland titles for Tipp.

PURPLE PATCH

If someone, especially a sports player or a sports team, goes through a period of time when everything seems to go right and they are very successful, they are said to have gone through a purple patch!

CORK 1975–79
Following their success in the 1950s, Cork would have to wait until the mid-1970s for their next golden era. They won five Munster titles in a row, in 1975–79, and three consecutive All-Irelands, but couldn't quite match the feats of Christy Ring & co.

GALWAY 1985–90
In 1980, Galway captain Joe Connolly made a famous speech when they won the All-Ireland. He sang 'The West's Awake' and declared 'People of Galway, we love you!' But that win wasn't backed up until 1987, with the emergence of another Joe – this time 22-year-old Joe Cooney, the star of the show. Galway won All-Irelands in 1987 and '88, but lost the 1990 final to Cork.

CLARE 1995–98
Ger Loughnane's team changed the game of hurling in the mid-1990s. The Banner had big, strong, tough players, and they won every physical battle – and a couple of All-Irelands too, in 1995 and 1997.

LIMERICK 2018–PRESENT
The latest purple patch belongs to John Kiely's Limerick team. They won the All-Ireland in 2018, and then managed four in a row in 2020–23.

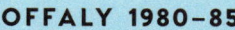

OFFALY 1980–85
For the faithful of Offaly, the 1980s were a special era. They won their first Leinster title in 1980 and by the end of the decade they had won five more! Their All-Ireland breakthrough came in 1981, which they followed up with a second title in 1985, beating a Galway side in both finals.

OFFALY 1994–98
Offaly kickstarted the revolution of the 1990s, which saw counties outside the Big Three win throughout the decade. They beat Limerick in '94 and qualified for the 1998 final via the 'back door'. In it, Offaly triumphed over Kilkenny, but the revolutionary years ended soon after and the Big Three dominated once again.

KILKENNY 2006–14
Perhaps the greatest team ever to grace a hurling field was Brian Cody's Kilkenny side. They were unstoppable – quite literally – between 2006 and 2009. The famous Drive-for-Five in 2010 ended in defeat to Tipperary, and to this day no hurling team has ever managed to win five All-Irelands in a row.

COUNTY HURLING KINGPINS

COUNTY	SENIOR ALL-IRELANDS WON
Kilkenny	36
Cork	30
Tipperary	28
Limerick	11
Wexford	6
Dublin	6

HURLING SUPER-CLUBS

CLUB	SENIOR ALL-IRELANDS WON
Ballyhale Shamrocks, Co. Kilkenny	9
Birr, Co. Offaly	4
Portumna, Co. Galway	4
Athenry, Co. Galway	3
Blackrock, Co. Cork	3
James Stephens, Co. Kilkenny	3

GIANTS OF THE GAME

SINCE HURLING IS an ancient sport, it's very hard to pick the best players of all time! Here are some of the most accomplished hurlers to ever strike a ball – from the great Christy Ring, who played during World War II, to Gemma O'Connor, who retired in 2021 with nine All-Ireland medals.

CHRISTY RING
CORK, 1939-62

This Cork legend is often said to be the greatest hurler of all time. Christy Ring's playing career lasted a remarkable 24 years – and he is still the only man to play at inter-county level across *four* decades! Known for his strength, bravery and scoring prowess, Ring was the ultimate hurler. He won eight All-Ireland titles and nine Munster titles.

EDDIE KEHER
KILKENNY, 1959-77

Known as 'Steady Eddie', Keher was central to the Kilkenny teams of the 1960s and '70s. He scored 35 goals and 336 points during his career – a record that stood until his countyman Henry Shefflin surpassed it in 2010. Eddie won six All-Irelands, five All-Stars and 10 Leinster titles.

NICKY RACKARD
WEXFORD, 1940-57

Another man who would challenge for the title of greatest ever hurler is Wexford legend Nicky Rackard. In fact, Rackard still holds the record for most goals scored in championship: 59! He inspired a breakthrough in the 1950s that saw Wexford crowned All-Ireland champions in 1955 and '56. Nicky's brothers Billy and Bobby were also on that team.

ANGELA AND ANN DOWNEY
KILKENNY, ANGELA (1970-95) AND ANN (1973-99)

Twin sisters Ann and Angela Downey each won 12 All-Ireland medals with Kilkenny, including the county's first ever senior title in 1974 – when they were only 17! The twins' telepathic awareness of one another on the field made them virtually unstoppable. Angela's lightning speed and eye for a goal changed the game of camogie, and she is often said to be the sport's best ever player.

EOIN KELLY
TIPPERARY, 2000-14

Tipperary have always produced brilliant hurlers, and one of the greatest ever forwards to come from Tipp was Eoin Kelly of Mullinahone. He played senior inter-county for 14 seasons, beginning when he was still a minor in 2000. Kelly scored a remarkable 21 goals and 367 points in 59 games. He won two All-Irelands and was captain of the 2010 team that denied Kilkenny a historic five in a row.

GEMMA O'CONNOR
CORK, 2002-21

With nine All-Ireland medals and ten All-Stars, Gemma O'Connor is the most successful player in the game. She played with Cork for 19 years, much of it in midfield, marshalling the players around her to success. A soldier in the defence forces, O'Connor was known for her incredible stamina – she was so fit, she'd cover just about every blade of grass in Croke Park during a match!

KEN MCGRATH
WATERFORD, 1996-2011

A talismanic half-back, Ken McGrath is widely recognised as one of the greatest hurlers never to win an All-Ireland. He could play anywhere around the middle of the field, from centre back to centre forward, and would pull the strings for the players around him. McGrath won four Munster titles, three All-Stars and was an All-Ireland runner up in 2008.

GEARÓID HEGARTY
LIMERICK, 2016-PRESENT

The Limerick team under John Kiely was – and still is! – full of incredible hurlers. Gearóid Hegarty epitomises the physicality and skill that this team plays with. Hegarty has helped the Treatymen become almost impossible to beat. In 2018, they won the All-Ireland for the first time since 1973!

LEGENDARY HURLING MANAGERS

GREAT LEADERS WILL always motivate others to perform, and hurling managers are no different. They listen to players, understand what makes them 'tick' and use that superpower to create a dressing-room environment that knows how to win ... and to lose!

BRIAN CODY
KILKENNY, 1998-2022

'ALL HURLERS ARE THE SAME. IF YOU COULD PLAY FOREVER, YOU WOULD.'

Brian Cody is broadly accepted as the GOAT (the Greatest of All Time). During his 24-year tenure, Kilkenny won 11 All-Irelands, including four in a row from 2006 to 2009. Cody's Cats also won 10 league titles during that time and 18 Leinster titles. There's a running joke in Kilkenny that Brian doesn't exist outside of a hurling pitch. Few people have ever seen him off it ...

LIAM GRIFFIN
WEXFORD, 1995-96

'I LOVED THE THINKING SIDE OF THE GAME AND I USED TO THINK THE GAME INSIDE OUT ALL MY LIFE ANYWAY.'

Under Griffin's leadership, Wexford came from nowhere to lift Liam MacCarthy in 1996 – for the first time since 1968. Griffin made all his players get off the bus on the way to Croke Park for a Leinster final against Offaly – he made them walk over the border out of Wexford and said, 'When we walk back into Wexford tonight, we'll have that Leinster Cup.'

DONAL O'GRADY
CORK, 2002-04

'THERE MAY BE PEOPLE THAT HAVE MORE TALENT THAN YOU, BUT THERE'S NO EXCUSE FOR ANYONE TO WORK HARDER THAN YOU DO.'

Being a manager in a time of disarray is a special skill. The Cork hurlers revolted against their county board in the mid-2000s. They believed they weren't being given the right support and resources. Donal O'Grady was their manager – and often the go-between! He had a brilliant hurling brain and built one of the teams of the century. He led them to win two All-Irelands in a row in 2004 and 2005.

JOHN KIELY
LIMERICK, 2016–PRESENT

'IT'S PART OF OUR IDENTITY, AND IF OUR IDENTITY CANNOT BE SEEN BY HOW WE PERFORM, WE'RE NOT PERFORMING AT ALL.'

Limerick are in a golden era right now, but that success began as far back as 2010, with the setting up of an underage development academy. The current senior team is the first full crop of graduates, and they have been flying high both at Munster and All-Ireland level. John Kiely became the Limerick senior manager in 2017. So far, they've won All-Irelands in 2018, 2020, 2021, 2022 and 2023!

GER LOUGHNANE
CLARE, 1994–2000

'SOME PEOPLE SAY HURLING ISN'T VERY IMPORTANT IN THE SCHEME OF THINGS. BUT TO HURLING PEOPLE HURLING IS THE SCHEME OF THINGS.'

Ger Loughnane brought an unprecedented level of fitness to the Clare hurlers in the mid-1990s. Both Anthony Daly and Davy Fitzgerald were managed by him! He brought them to the sand dunes of West Clare at dawn and made them run up and down them … and it worked! Under Loughnane, Clare won every physical battle on the field and two All-Ireland titles, in 1995 and 1997.

THE GENERATIONAL MANAGER

Some managers have gone back to do the same job twice, sometimes years apart. They couldn't say no to another crack of the whip!

CYRIL FARRELL
GALWAY
1979–82, 1984–91 and again in 1996–98

JUSTIN MCCARTHY
CORK
1975–76 and again in 1984–85

MICHAEL 'BABS' KEATING
TIPPERARY
1987–94 and again in 2006–07

LIAM SHEEDY
TIPPERARY
2008–10 and again in 2019–21

DAVY FITGERALD
WATERFORD
2008–11 and again in 2022–present

POC FADA

THE POC FADA is a hurling and camogie specialty. It's also a great example of the close ties between Gaelic games and the Irish language – *poc fada* translates as 'long puck' *as Gaeilge*, which explains the game and the competition perfectly! The Poc Fada All-Ireland Championships are held every year and test the skills and strength of the top hurlers and camógs in Ireland. It involves pucking your way around a hilly course in the Cooley Mountains.

RULES OF THE GAME

Contestants must puck a sliotar, using a hurl, and the winner is the player who needs the lowest number of pucks to move the sliotar around the course and get to the finish line!

Players can either lift and strike or hit the ball directly from the hand. If two players take the same number of pucks, the winner is determined by how far their ball has gone over the finish line. The best players are often goalkeepers because they are used to driving the sliotar far up the field on a puck-out!

THE HISTORY

The very first Poc Fada was played in 1960. Two men – Oliver Hodgers and An tAthair Pól Mac Seáin – laid out a 5km course around the Cooley Mountains in Co. Louth. The course ran from An Céide on Annaverna Mountain to the fields of the Mills family in Aghameen. Although the course has changed since then, the wild Cooley Mountains are still home to the event. Smaller Poc Fada competitions are often run by local GAA clubs along rural roads and fields.

KINGS AND QUEENS

Following that first Poc Fada competition, the GAA quickly organised the first All-Ireland competition – just one year later! An All-Ireland hurling and camogie Poc Fada champion is crowned every year in August, as well as an under-16 champion. The winners are aptly referred to as the King or the Queen of the Mountain.

YOUNG POCS

Do people tell you that you've a 'great belt of a ball'? Well maybe the Poc Fada is for you. Did you know there is a boys' under-16 and a girls' under-16 All-Ireland Poc Fada championship? Why not ask your club about the competition and work towards being crowned King or Queen of the Mountain one day. Make sure to use your goalkeeper's hurl with the bigger bas!

DID YOU KNOW?

Legend has it that Cú Chulainn took this route through the mountains on his way to a feast. But, on the long and lonely journey, Cú Chulainn got bored. So he decided to hit a sliotar in front of him and run ahead to catch it – and that's where the idea for the Poc Fada comes from. Thanks, Cú Chulainn!

PLAYER PROFILES

BRENDAN CUMMINS

TIPPERARY GOALKEEPER
Nine-time champion
2004, '06, ' 07, '08, '11, '12, '13, '14, '15

PATRICIA JACKMAN

WATERFORD MIDFIELDER
Seven-time champion
2009, '10, '11, '12, '13, '14, '15

GAA HANDBALL

HANDBALL IS *FAST*, and it's this speed that makes the sport so much fun to play – and to watch! But the best thing about it? All you need is a wall and a ball!

GRAB A WALL, A BALL AND ...

Handball is an ancient Gaelic sport. There are local, provincial and All-Ireland championships, just like in hurling and football. The aim of the game is to hit the ball with the palm of your hand off the front wall, and then let it bounce twice before your opponent can return it. You have to be super fit and coordinated to follow the little ball as it flies around the alley!

THE HISTORY OF HANDBALL

The Irish Handball Council was set up in 1924, and it was then that handball took off. Throughout the 1900s, handball alleys sprung up all over the country and became focal points in Irish society. Children and adults would meet at the local alley for a chat or a quick match. The sport enjoyed huge popularity from the 1940s to the '70s and '80s. This popularity culminated in a groundbreaking TV show called *Top Ace*, which showed the fast-paced sport in colour for the first time. Handball isn't as popular today as it was then, but it has continued to thrive in pockets around the country.

DID YOU KNOW?

Hurling legend D.J. Carey said that playing handball made him a better hurler: 'My footwork and anticipation came from handball. The game of handball stood to me more than anything in the game of hurling.'

WHAT'S THE DIFFERENCE?

There are two types of Gaelic handball in Ireland: hardball and softball. Hardball is faster and is considered the original form of the game. Softball is played in a bigger alley and was traditionally played in the summer months because the courts were outdoors.

Internationally, there is also One-Wall and Four-Wall handball. The One-Wall game is the most prestigious, and world championships are held every year with competitors from Ireland, Europe, Canada and the US. The 2012 World Championships were held in Dublin.

BALL ALLEY BIG SHOTS!

There have been many famous Irish world handball champions. Have you heard of any of them?

PAUL BRADY

Paul Brady was a talented footballer, but he was first and foremost an international handball superstar. Brady won every All-Ireland senior championship singles title from 2003 to 2013, bar one. He also won a remarkable *five* world titles between 2003 and 2015. He was a clever, focused operator who was rarely caught out.

MICHAEL 'DUCKSIE' WALSH

Ducksie was the first handball hero the country had ever heard of. He won eight All-Ireland senior championship singles titles from 1986 to 1998, and teamed up with Michael Reade to win the doubles! Later he played alongside his friend, Kilkenny hurler D.J. Carey, and together they won three senior All-Irelands.

FIONA SHANNON

Fiona Shannon, from St Paul's Club, Belfast, is a three-time world champion and a household name for handball fans. She holds a record nine All-Ireland singles titles and eight All-Ireland doubles championships with various partners, including her sister Sibéal. When Shannon retired, the next big superstar also came from St Paul's: a young Aisling Reilly.

GAA ROUNDERS

GAA ROUNDERS IS a bat and ball game, and it's a great sport to play if you want to get fit and develop keen hand–eye coordination! It was the fourth official Gaelic game included in the original GAA charter of 1884, along with hurling, handball and Gaelic football.

HEY, BATTER, BATTER, SWING!

GAA rounders is believed to be one of the origins for baseball. Historians believe that Irish immigrants brought the game with them to the US – and in the 1800s, a lot of the top baseball players were either Irish or of Irish descent. Back then, baseball was much more like rounders, with underarm pitching and no gloves. Both games still have a pitcher and a batter and four bases. The term 'home run' is also used in both!

ON THE BALL

Unlike in hurling, camogie and Gaelic football, GAA rounders is a mixed team sport, meaning that men and women can play on the same team. A team consists of nine players and the game is played with a round bat – not a hurl! – and a sliotar. GAA rounders is played at club level rather than inter-county, but the teams all have their own club colours and jerseys. There is even an All-Ireland Championship played every year!

DID YOU KNOW?

Paul 'The Gunner' Brady played football for Cavan and is regarded as Ireland's greatest-ever handball player. He was so multi-talented that he also played for Erne Eagles, a GAA rounders team that won 10 All-Irelands in a row! If he's not a dual player, does that make him a triad?!

HOW TO PLAY

A run is scored when a batter has tagged all three field bases before touching home base. There are 25m between each base – that's a total of 100m for a home run! The aim of the game is for the batting team to score as many runs as possible before the fielding team get three players out. A batter can be out for a number of reasons: if they fail to strike their third good ball, if they strike the last good ball into foul ground, if they strike a good ball but it is caught by a fielder, or if their base is tagged by a fielder before they reach it.

THIRD BASE

SECOND BASE
The fielding team try to gain possession of the ball and throw it to a 'base minder' at first, second or third base.

PITCHER
The pitcher stands facing home base. They deliver the ball underarm to the batter.

FOUL LINES
The batter must hit inside the foul lines for the ball to remain in play.

BATTER
The batter strikes the ball forward into the field of play. Once the batter hits the ball, they can run to first base.

FIRST BASE

HOME BASE

CATCHER
The pitcher and catcher must wear GAA-approved helmets while fielding.

SPOTLIGHT ON THE KING: HENRY SHEFFLIN

HENRY SHEFFLIN IS widely regarded as the greatest hurler of all time – even outside Kilkenny! He is known as 'the King'. A leader on and off the field, Henry won every personal honour in the game, as well as a whopping 10 All-Ireland medals. He also won 3 All-Ireland club titles as a player with Ballyhale, before going on to win as their manager in 2019!

Hurling was in Henry's blood. He grew up in Ballyhale, a small village near the Kilkenny–Waterford border. Everybody in Ballyhale lives and breathes hurling. His dad was a selector with Kilkenny and had been a good hurler in his day. Henry was the youngest of seven – four boys and three girls! As soon as he could walk, he was out practising with his brothers in the yard behind his dad's pub.

Henry went to St Kieran's secondary school in Kilkenny. Kieran's is famous for producing top-quality hurlers, and a lot of Kilkenny's most successful players went there.

When Henry was at Kieran's, the star player was D.J. Carey – who went on to be a leader for the Kilkenny senior team. All the younger students looked up to D.J. and wanted to hurl as skilfully as the artful 'Dodger' one day.

Henry came to Kieran's as a very strong club player, but he was suddenly swallowed up among some of the best hurlers in the county and wasn't the standout player anymore! He worked hard to compete, but it just goes to show, you can go on to be the best player of a generation without starring as a juvenile. Keep working hard and you'll be rewarded. (We can't promise you'll win 10 All-Ireland medals, though – we can't all be royalty!)

Henry had talent, and he worked hard. He was also tall – he would grow to be six feet two inches! Even so, he had his fair share of injuries. In fifth year of St Kieran's he broke his toe (but still managed to play in an All-Ireland final less than two months later). Since then, he's suffered two cruciate knee ligament injuries, a broken foot, ripped cartilage in his shoulder, ruptured ankle ligaments and stress fractures ... No one said being the King was easy!

After he retired, Henry admitted that the title 'the King' didn't always sit well with him. When he was growing up, the Ballyhale hurlers were his heroes. The famous Fennelly brothers – all seven of them – played and won stacks of All-Ireland medals with Ballyhale. Those men were the kings in Henry's eyes, and they left their egos at the door.

Henry may think he doesn't deserve to be called The King, but hurling people don't anoint royalty lightly! Another hurling legend, Brian Cody, once said this about Henry: 'He got the absolute maximum. You talk about emptying the tank every so often on the pitch, but Henry emptied it all the time, and emptied it throughout his career, and that's a hell of a tribute to pay to anybody.'

THE KING'S PLAYING HONOURS:

COUNTY:
KILKENNY

ALL IRELANDS:
10

NATIONAL LEAGUES:
6

LEINSTER:
13

ALL-STAR AWARDS:
11

CLUB:
BALLYHALE

ALL IRELANDS:
3

LEINSTER:
4

KILKENNY:
6

THE BIG BALL

IF HURLING IS known among Gaels as the small ball, the sport of Gaelic football is often referred to as … yes, you've guessed it, the big ball! It is one of the four sports listed by the Gaelic Athletic Association upon its foundation in 1884, but Gaelic football is an ancient Irish game that has been played in various forms for centuries.

Unlike soccer, the ball can be lifted and kicked from the ground or the hands. It can be bounced and handpassed too. Gaelic football is played by teams of 15, who must amass the highest score with points and goals. All the counties in Ireland play in the Men's National League and Championship – except Kilkenny! Gaelic football is played by both men and women, but the two games have very slight differences. The GAA governs the men's game and the LGFA is in charge of the women's. The Sam Maguire Cup and the Brendan Martin Cup are the holy grails of intercounty football.

Some Gaelic footballers have even switched to the Australian Football League and earn a living from playing the sport. A hybrid version of the sport, called 'International Rules', is played against Australia, giving Irish Gaelic footballers a chance to represent their country on a world stage. Read on to learn all about the special place Gaelic football has in the lives of Irish people at home and abroad!

GAELIC FOOTBALL

HISTORIANS AGREE THAT the ancient sport of Gaelic football is older than soccer and rugby, but the exact date of its origin is unclear. There are records of a version of Gaelic football being played as far back as the 14th century.

THE GAME

Gaelic football is probably the most popular Gaelic game. Unlike soccer, the ball can be handled, and the skills for Gaelic football are transferable to sports like basketball and rugby. Scores are counted in points and goals (which are worth 3 points). Senior matches last 70 minutes, with two halves of 35 minutes.

STARTER'S ORDERS!

The positions on the field of play for football are the same as those for hurling. There are 15 players on each team – 14 outfield and 1 goalie. What's your favourite position?

DID YOU KNOW?

Lots of famous people have tried out Gaelic football. Have you heard of the Spanish football legend Xabi Alonso? Well, when he was 15, he spent the summer in Kells, Co. Meath. He was in Ireland to study English – but was also introduced to Gaelic football!

44

SKILLS ZONE

When you first join your club's academy or nursery, you will learn the key skills of Gaelic football. Have you perfected all these skills?

CROUCH PICK-UP

Move towards the ball, bending down at the hips and knees. Place your hands in front of the ball, with your fingers spread out. Boys need to bring their toe to the ball before picking it up, but girls can pick it straight up off the ground. Draw the ball into your body, and you're ready to solo, handpass or kick.

SOLO

You can take four steps with the ball in hand before you need to either pass it, bounce it on the ground or take a solo or 'toe tap'. You drop the ball to your foot, flick the toe upwards keeping your leg straight, and the ball bounces upwards towards your body!

HANDPASS

The handpass is used to pass the ball across short distances. You cup or support the ball in the palm of your non-dominant hand, and use your dominant hand to swing backwards and then follow through as you strike the ball in the direction you need the ball to go.

PUNT KICK

This kick is the most common kick pass in Gaelic football and can also be used to score a goal if the target is straight in front of you. Drop the ball to your kicking foot, and kick with the in-step. Follow through, pointing your toe in the direction you want the ball to go!

HIGH CATCH

This is a very important skill, because it's used to win possession from a kick-out or to claim a mark. You move towards the ball, jumping off one foot and swinging the other leg. Extend your arms up over your head, and make a 'V' shape with your two hands. Remember to keep your eyes on the ball. Move the ball into your chest as soon as you catch it!

HOOK KICK

The hook kick is used for kicking points or if you need to pass the ball to a teammate at an angle. You release the ball and kick with the inside of the foot, following through with your toe pointing upwards.

DECADES AND DYNASTIES

REACHING AN ALL-IRELAND final is a huge achievement, and the players involved become heroes of their generation. Here is a look at some of the winning trends in Gaelic football.

HEAVYWEIGHT OR ONE-HIT WONDER?

Gaelic football success comes in waves, especially for the traditional powerhouses of the game. When a county like Kerry wins an All-Ireland, you can be almost certain they will put two titles back-to-back. The Kingdom have won a minimum of two in a row *four* times in the last half a century or so.

For most counties, winning *one* All-Ireland is the ultimate dream. Sometimes, there's an exciting 'flash in the pan'. Armagh and Derry have won the Sam Maguire Cup only once, and the celebrations went on for months. I bet nobody in those counties got homework that September!

1940s
In 1947, Cavan beat Kerry in the All-Ireland final, which was held at the Polo Grounds in New York! It's the only All-Ireland final to be played *outside* Ireland.

1960s
Down and Galway were the most successful teams of the 1960s. Down won two in a row in 1960 and 1961, and Galway won three in a row from 1964 to 1966.

1950s
Cavan stopped Mayo from claiming three in a row in 1952, and Mayo haven't won another title since. During the 1950s, the Sam Maguire Cup was won by seven different counties. This kind of spread wouldn't happen again for another 40 years.

1970s
Gaelic football enjoyed an exciting revival in the 1970s. It became 'cool' and even overtook sports like soccer in terms of popularity. Heffo's Army was a large part of that in the capital city. After an 11-year drought, Kevin Heffernan's Dubs won three All-Ireland's in four years, from 1974 to 1977. Offaly were the flash in the pan of the 1970s, winning Sam Maguire in 1971 and '72.

1980s

From 1974 to 1986, either Kerry or Dublin won the All-Ireland every year – except in 1982, when Séamus Darby's famous goal for Offaly denied Kerry the five in a row. The Kingdom were by far the greatest team of this decade.

2000s

After some time to rebuild during the 1990s, Kerry's inevitable revival came – but they didn't have it all their own way in the 2000s. Tyrone were the stand-out team of this decade, and they enjoyed a healthy rivalry with both Dublin and Kerry. They won the All-Ireland in 2003, 2005 and 2008! The flash in the pan during this decade was Armagh in 2002. This was the only time they've ever won the All-Ireland! Kerry were back, though, winning in '04, '06, '07 and '09.

2020s

Who will claim the 2020s? Dublin, Tyrone and Kerry are the early contenders!

1990s

In the late 1980s and early 1990s, Cork and Meath enjoyed purple patches as the Kerry machine went into decline. In 1990, Cork even won the double. (That's when the hurling and football All-Irelands are won by the same county in the same year.) But then the Ulster counties enjoyed a renaissance. Down won in 1991 and '94, Donegal in 1992 and Derry in 1993. In 1995, Tyrone were beaten in the final by Dublin, who hadn't won an All-Ireland since 1983. In 1998, there was a novel final pairing when Galway beat Kildare.

2010s

In 2010, Cork beat Down in the All-Ireland final to win their first title since 1990. 2011 gave us a glimpse of what was to come from the Dubs. They beat Kerry in 2011 and Mayo in 2013 … and then went on to win a record *six* All-Ireland titles in a row from 2015 to 2020. Managed by Jim Gavin, this team of stars became the greatest ever collection of players to play the game. Meanwhile, Mayo are still chasing that elusive next title – they still haven't won since 1951!

LADIES' FOOTBALL

LADIES' GAELIC FOOTBALL is just that – Gaelic football for women and girls. Like camogie, ladies' football didn't feature when the GAA was being set up, as women didn't have the same status as men in 1884. Nowadays, though, ladies' football is one of the fastest-growing sports in Europe!

FROM HISTORY TO HEADLINES

It wasn't until the 1960s that a 'new craze' took hold of sports-mad women in Ireland. Other field team games like camogie and hockey were already popular, but for women to encroach on the men's game of Gaelic football was unheard of! The 1960s was a decade of rebellion, and playing Gaelic football was just one of the many barriers that women began to break down. Small, local tournaments were set up in rural parts of Offaly and Tipperary, and by the early 1970s the game began to make newspaper headlines for the first time.

RULE MAKERS

In 1974, the Ladies Gaelic Football Association was set up in the same hotel as the GAA a century before – Lizzy Hayes' Hotel in Thurles. There were representatives from just four counties: Offaly, Tipperary, Kerry and Galway. These counties had begun the revolution and introduced local football fairs and competitions for women. The LGFA wrote down the rules for ladies' football and put structures in place similar to the GAA and the Camogie Association, like clubs and county boards.

LGFA TODAY

Today, ladies' football is thriving not just in Ireland, but in Europe, Asia, America and beyond. There are 1,016 clubs in Ireland, with more than 163,873 registered players, and huge crowds attend the All-Ireland final day at Croke Park. Many of Ireland's inter-county stars have gone on to play Aussie Rules football professionally in Australia. There are lots of great ways to get involved in playing ladies' football at any age. Have you heard of Gaelic4Teens or even Gaelic4Mothers&Others?

RULE DIFFERENCES

The rules are very similar to the men's game with a few slight variations. For example, in men's Gaelic football, players give away a free kick if they pick the ball up off the ground without putting a foot to it, but in ladies' football the clean pick-up is allowed. Here are some of the other key differences.

LADIES' GAELIC FOOTBALL	MEN'S GAELIC FOOTBALL
Clean pick-up	Foot-to-ball pick-up
Shoulder-to-shoulder challenge disallowed	Shoulder-to-shoulder challenge allowed
Kick-out from 20m line	Kick-out from 13m line
First infraction – yellow card and sin bin	First infraction – a booking only, no card
Red card for pulling another player's hair	No such rule
60-minute game	70-minute game
Size 4 football	Size 5 football
30 players on a panel	24 players on a panel

GIANTS OF THE GAME

HAVE YOU AND your friends ever tried to decide who is the best footballer in the country? Now try to figure out if the best footballer of today would beat the best footballer of 1982. Impossible, right? It's very difficult to compare one great defender with the best goalie to ever stand between the posts. But here are some of the best-loved Gaelic football players ever.

PAT SPILLANE
KERRY, 1974–91

The Kingdom of Kerry produced most of the top-class footballers for a very long time, and Pat Spillane of Templenoe is regarded as one of the best ever players of the game. Over the course of a 17-year playing career, he won eight All-Irelands and nine All-Stars.

SUE RAMSBOTTOM
LAOIS, 1988–2003

A Laois powerhouse right throughout the 1990s, Sue played in and lost *six* All-Ireland finals before finally winning one in 2001. Despite the missed medals during that decade, Sue won seven All-Stars during her 15-year career with Laois. Not unlike the great Mayo footballer Cora Staunton, Sue played senior football aged 12!

TEDDY MCCARTHY
CORK, 1985–96

Known for his high fielding, Teddy McCarthy was a key player on Billy Morgan's Cork football team of the late '80s and early '90s. He could just as easily sit on the Giants of Hurling page because he won two All-Ireland medals in both codes! He even did double in 1990. 'Teddy Mac' passed away in 2023.

PETER CANAVAN
TYRONE, 1989–2005

A key cog in the Mickey Harte Tyrone team of the mid-2000s, Peter Canavan is one of the most decorated Ulster footballers ever. He was voted an All-Star on six occasions despite 'only' winning the All-Ireland twice, in 2003 and 2005.

FUN FACT

Lee Keegan is the highest-scoring defender of all time, clocking up 6–40 in 54 championship matches with an overall tally for Mayo of 8–71 … from the backs!

CORA STAUNTON
MAYO, 1995–2018

A footballing prodigy, Cora played her first senior football match for Mayo at the age of 13 (which wouldn't be allowed now, before you get any ideas!) and has won four All-Irelands. She's also won six club All-Irelands with Carnacon. Since 2018, she has built a reputation in the Australian Rules women's football league as one of the all-time greatest goalkickers.

STEPHEN CLUXTON
DUBLIN, 2001–PRESENT

Stephen Cluxton is possibly the best footballing mind ever to take to the field – and he's a goalkeeper! He pulled the strings from between the posts for the hugely successful Dublin team that won six in a row. His game-management and kick-out strategies have become the stuff of legend.

MICHAEL MURPHY
DONEGAL, 2007–22

When Michael Murphy came along, Donegal started doing well. Michael, who is from Glenswilly, was named captain for the 2011 season at the tender age of 21, and a year later led from the front in Donegal's All-Ireland final success against Mayo. He played a talismanic role for Donegal until 2022.

DAVID CLIFFORD
KERRY, 2018–PRESENT

Born in 1999, David Clifford is only getting started, but already football people say he's overtaken *everyone* as the best ever player of Gaelic football. So far, he's got one All-Ireland for Kerry and a legion of fans nationwide ... watch this space!

WIDE OF THE MARK ...

These are some of the greatest footballers never to win an All-Ireland.

DERMOT EARLEY SR
Roscommon
Midfield
All-Irelands 0
Connacht 5
All-Stars 2

DECLAN BROWNE
Tipperary
Forward
All-Irelands 0
Munster 0
All-Stars 2

EUGENE 'NUDIE' HUGHES
Monaghan
Forward
All-Irelands 0
Ulster 3
All-Stars 3

LEE KEEGAN
Mayo
Defender
All-Irelands 0
Connacht 7
All-Stars 5

FAMOUS FOOTBALL RIVALRIES

RIVALRIES EXIST IN every walk of life, but there is something almost electric about sporting rivalries. When you beat your closest rival, the spark of joy at the final whistle is like a current of positive energy running through your body. When you lose, it's almost like you've been plugged out!

DERBY DUELS AND FRIENDLY FOES

Have you ever heard the phrase 'Keep your friends close, and your enemies closer?' Some of the keenest rivalries in sport occur between the teams closest to one another. It probably happens in your Cumann na mBunscol and Go Games matches too. Games against the nearest rival club or school are always the spiciest, aren't they?

BITTER GAELIC GAMES RIVALRIES

KERRY VS DUBLIN

The Dublin vs Kerry rivalry is probably the greatest in Gaelic football – and maybe even in Gaelic games. The two counties always seem to find form at the same time, and it can result in half a dozen years of entertainment every two decades or so.

The Kerry/Dublin matchups of the late 1970s are infamous. Kevin Heffernan was one of the most charismatic managers ever, and he was well matched by Mick O'Dwyer. Heffo's Army won the All-Ireland in 1974, beating Galway in the final. Not only were Dublin a flashy football team, they were adored by the media and built up as the team to beat. Kerry took the bait, and what followed was a game of cat and mouse, as the two teams battled it out in four of the next six All-Irelands.

DUBLIN VS MEATH

Dublin didn't have to wait long for their next big rivalry – and it came from much closer to home! Seán Boylan took over the Meath footballers in 1982, and by '86 they were more than a match for the Dubs. Meath went on to win All-Irelands in '87 and '88, but the rivalry was sharpest in 1991, when a preliminary Leinster Championship match had to be played *four times* to find a winner. (Meath won by a point!)

GALWAY VS MAYO

Did you know Galway won the 1998 All-Ireland with a Mayo man – John O'Mahony – as manager? What made it worse was that Mayo had lost the 1996 and 1997 All-Ireland finals. Mayo took great comfort in knocking Galway out of the championship the following year. Because the players in Galway and Mayo often attend school or college together, the rivalry is traditionally a very friendly one ... But once the ball is thrown in, friendships are left to one side and football foes are born!

TYRONE VS ARMAGH

Even though Tyrone and Armagh enjoyed a sparky relationship for decades, this derby had an added level of intrigue in 2002 and 2003. Armagh had never won the All-Ireland until they lifted Sam Maguire in 2002, and beating Tyrone in the Ulster Championship earlier that summer had been key in reaching the holy grail. A year later, Tyrone's revenge was sweet when they won the All-Ireland, beating Armagh in the final.

CORK VS KERRY

As much as you might think you can't stand the sight of your rivals, would your team be as strong without the healthy competition? Probably not. That's how Pat Spillane summed up the Cork vs Kerry rivalry of the 1970s and '80s. Even though Kerry were the team to beat, and tussled with Dublin for All-Ireland honours, it was in Munster finals against Cork that they were pushed to the pin of their collar.

BRILLIANT BAINISTEOIRÍ

WITH A HISTORY so rich, Gaelic football has produced some of the longest-serving and most successful managers of almost any sport in the world. Here is a selection of the greatest ever *bainisteoirí*!

MICK O'DWYER
KERRY, 1975-89

'I'M TOTALLY ADDICTED TO THE GAME ... I'LL KEEP AT IT UNTIL I GO INTO THE GRAVE.'

Known affectionately as 'Micko', Mick O'Dwyer will go down in history as the GOAT – the Greatest of All Time. He guided the Kingdom to eight All-Irelands, and also brought his Midas touch to Laois, Kildare and Wicklow. Once, on a team holiday in San Francisco in 1987, the famous Kerry team had been partying too hard and were badly beaten in an exhibition match. That afternoon, Micko brought them to a local beach and made them do a running session in the sand ... in the off season ... on their holidays!

JOHN O'MAHONY
MAYO, 1987-91 & 2007-10
LEITRIM, 1993-95
GALWAY 1997-2004

'WINNING IS LINKED TO POSITIVITY, IT'S NOT COMFORTABLE TO BE POSITIVE NOW [AFTER A DEFEAT] BUT WE HAVE TO BE, WE DON'T HAVE A CHOICE.'

John O'Mahony is a proud Mayo man, but his success as a manager came with the Tribesmen. He was the Galway boss in the late 1980s and even though he led them to an All-Ireland final in 1989 it wasn't deemed a successful stint by the harsh critics in Galway! He came back a few years later and brought not one but two All-Ireland football titles to Galway, in 1998 and 2001. They haven't won it since!

BILLY MORGAN
CORK, 1986-96 & 2003-7

'IF THE PASSION WASN'T THERE, IT'S TIME TO GO.'

Billy Morgan took over in 1986 and within seven years the Rebels had reached five All-Ireland finals, winning two. Morgan was a passionate club man too, and managed his club Nemo Rangers after he finished with the Cork footballers. In 2003, Nemo won the Club All-Ireland, and the county board asked Morgan to take over the Cork senior team again. Off he went and won *another* All-Ireland title with them in 2007. Success follows the best in the business around!

MICKEY HARTE
TYRONE, 2003–20
LOUTH, 2021–PRESENT

'IF IT DOESN'T MEAN THAT MUCH TO YOU, WELL THEN: MAYBE YOU SHOULD BE DOING SOMETHING ELSE.'

Mickey Harte's success began when his core crop of players were still teenagers. He began with the Tyrone minors in 1991, then managed the under-21s, before guiding the same group of players to All-Ireland success later in their careers. Harte redefined the art of defending, and that's how Tyrone built a legacy, winning All-Irelands in 2003, 2005 and 2008.

KEVIN HEFFERNAN
DUBLIN, 1974–76 & 1978–86

'WHAT WE WENT THROUGH TOGETHER WAS DEEPER THAN JUST FOOTBALL.'

'Heffo's Army' was beloved in the capital, and probably reluctantly admired all over the country too. They made Gaelic football cool in the 1970s. Heffo was a larger-than-life character and is remembered for the legacy he left as much as for the three All-Irelands his team won in 1974, 1976 and 1983. He was a leader who taught his players how to carry success with humility and to celebrate the team before the individual.

SEÁN BOYLAN
MEATH, 1982–2005

'I ALWAYS SAID, THERE IS A CERTAIN MADNESS IN MEATH FOOTBALL. YOU CAN'T TAKE THAT OUT OF US.'

Seán Boylan's success was extra special because he was in charge for so long. He rebuilt his starting 15 at least three times. During the two decades he was Meath boss, the team was feared and admired in equal measure for their physicality, tenacity and ruthlessness. Boylan, who was originally a hurling man, won All-Ireland football titles with Meath in 1986, 1987, 1996 and 1999.

AUSSIE RULES

AUSSIE RULES – or 'footy' as it's known down under – is the most popular team sport in Australia. The game was originally invented for cricket players to keep in shape during the off season! It's a very similar game to Gaelic football in that you can pick up the ball and kick it from the hand.

THE RULES

In Aussie Rules 'footy', not only is the ball oval shaped but so is the field! Instead of two halves, there are four quarters of 20 minutes each in a match, so fitness levels are very high indeed. You can kick or hand pass the ball to your teammates, and if a player makes a clean catch from a kick pass they can claim a 'mark' and take a free kick. At each end of the pitch, there are four upright poles. A goal is a kick between the two middle posts and is worth six points. If the ball goes wide of the centre posts, but inside the outer posts, the score is called a 'behind' and is worth just one point. Imagine getting a point for kicking the ball 'wide' in Gaelic football!

WINNERS AND LOSERS

Do you know what a wooden spoon is? Well, it's an imaginary 'award' handed down to the team that finishes last in the AFL league. St Kilda have the most wooden spoon awards, with 27, while Adelaide is the only AFL team that has avoided 'winning' a wooden spoon! You might have heard that the Rugby 6 Nations Championship also uses the term 'wooden spoon' for the team that finishes lowest in the table.

THE STARS

Lots of Irish footballers have made a home in Australia. They often live there for a few years and playing football is their job. You can get paid to play in Australia because, unlike Gaelic games, it is a professional sport.

JIM STYNES

Jim Stynes was the original convert. He switched permanently from a Dublin senior footballer to an Australian Rules player for Melbourne in 1987. He went on to become the first and only non-Aussie-born player to win the Brownlow Medal, which is a bit like Footballer of the Year in Gaelic games.

TADHG KENNELLY

Tadhg Kennelly grew up playing football with Listowel Emmets in Kerry but in 2001 travelled to play footy with the Sydney Swans. In 2005, he became the first Irishman to win an AFL Premiership title. In 2009, he decided to come home for a season and won an All-Ireland with Kerry! He is the only person to win both an All-Ireland Senior Football Championship and an AFL Premiership title.

ZACH TUOHY

This Laois man is considered one of the greatest ever Irish players in the AFL. Zach Tuohy, who plays with Geelong Football Club, has played the most matches of any non-Australian player in history. In 2022, Tuohy, along with Mark O'Connor from Kerry, won the AFL Grand Final with the Geelong Cats.

ORLA O'DWYER

Is there nothing Orla O'Dwyer can't do? A native of Cahir in County Tipperary, Orla grew up playing camogie and ladies' football. In 2020, she joined the Brisbane Lions AFLW team as an 'other-sport' rookie. In 2021, she won the Premiership title with the Lions and a year later became the first Irish woman to be named on the All-Australian Team of the Year.

INTERNATIONAL RULES

THE GAME OF International Rules is the only way to represent your country in Gaelic football ... or a version of it anyway! It's a hybrid game made up of Gaelic football and the Australian equivalent ('Aussie Rules'). It is held every year (although there have been some years which went unscheduled), and the two nations take turns hosting the event.

THE HISTORY

The Australian Football League (AFL) is the governing body for Australian Football 'down under'. The idea for an international series came from their first Australian Football World Tour, which took place in the late 1960s. A group of Aussie Rules stars played matches in Ireland using modified Gaelic football rules. The first official International Rules series took place in Ireland in 1984.

HOW DOES IT WORK?

The GAA and the AFL select a management team, and a squad of roughly 25 top players are selected from each country for the International Rules series. Two matches, known as 'tests', are played, and the highest total score determines the winners. There are two special medals awarded after each series, one for the best Irish player (the GAA Medal) and one for the best Australian (the Jim Stynes Medal). In 2004, the trophy presented to the winning team was named the Cormac McAnallen Cup, after a former International Rules and Tyrone All-Star.

IRELAND
V
AUSTRALIA

DID YOU KNOW?
A women's International Rules Series was held once in 2006, and a boys' event was also staged for eight years from 1999 to 2006. Would you like to see those competitions revived?

SPOT THE DIFFERENCE

When it came to the rules of the game, the two sports had to meet somewhere in the middle. Thankfully, the GAA managed to keep the round football. It was assumed (and rightly so!) that it would be too difficult for the Irish players to get used to kicking the Australians' oval ball, and the games wouldn't be competitive enough. The term 'behind' is a score worth one point, though in Gaelic games it would be a wide! Aussie Rules is more physical, and more aggressive tackling is allowed. Here are some more differences between the two games.

GAELIC FOOTBALL	INTERNATIONAL RULES	AUSTRALIAN FOOTBALL
H posts	H posts + 2 extra uprights	4 uprights
Rectangular pitch	Rectangular pitch	Oval pitch
Round football	Round football	Oval football
Goal worth 3　Point worth 1	Goal worth 6　Over (point) worth 3　Behind worth 1	Goal worth 6　Behind worth 1
Goal net	Goal net	No goal net
GAA-style jersey	GAA-style jersey	Sleeveless jersey
15 players on a team	15 players on a team	18 players on a team
2 halves of 30 minutes	4 quarters of 18 minutes	4 quarters of 20 minutes
'Throw-in'	'Throw-in'	'Ball up'

CATCH ME IF YOU CAN!

One of Ireland's fastest ever players on an International Rules pitch was a little Jack Russell who invaded the pitch during the 2004 match at Croke Park. Every time one of the players tried to catch him he escaped and tore off again. The match was stopped for two and half minutes and even the TV match commentator started describing the canine action!

SPOTLIGHT ON: RENA BUCKLEY

RENA BUCKLEY IS a dual player and multiple All-Star in both codes who set the world of Gaelic games alight. Of the 18 senior All-Ireland medals she picked up during her career, 11 were for football.

Rena grew up in a small place called Berrings in Co. Cork. She played camogie for Inniscarra and football for Donoughmore. When she was in primary school she played on the same team as her older brother, and one time in a big important match, she passed the ball to a 6th class boy on her team so that he could shoot for goal. He missed, and her brother scolded her for not taking the shot herself! She was only in 2nd class and started to realise she might be a very good footballer indeed!

Between 2003 and 2016, she also played for the Cork ladies' football team. Do you know that now nobody under the age of 17 can play senior inter-county football? When Rena started playing for Cork she was only 16, and she had two All-Ireland medals and an All-Star before she even left school! Her team, managed by Éamonn Ryan, became a force to be reckoned with, winning 11 All-Irelands in the space of 12 years.

Rena was the captain in 2012, so she got to climb the steps of the Hogan Stand and make a speech. Her parents always spoke a bit of Irish at home. Growing up, she said if she ever got the chance, she would make her speech *as Gaeilge*. When the time came, she was true to her word. She repeated that in 2017 when she captained the Cork camogie team to All-Ireland success. Again, that was a first – before Rena, nobody had ever managed to captain their home county to the greatest glory in the game across both codes.

When she was a child, she would run around the garden playing football and hurling, jumping up for high balls, pretending to be Teddy McCarthy, the great Cork dual star of the 1990 double. It was her dream to be a dual player for Cork, so sometimes dreams do come true!

Rena was a hard-working footballer, and playing at midfield, she often dominated the games she lined out in. She had some brilliant players around her like Bríd Stack, Angela Walsh and Briege Corkery – Corkery was another exceptional dual star for Cork, matching Buckley's 18 All-Irelands. That special Cork football team won five in a row between 2005 and 2009 and then six in a row from 2011 to 2016. Beating Dublin by a point in 2014 was one of Rena's career highlights. She said: 'We shouldn't have won, yet somehow we did … That was our Cork team. By then we had forgotten how to lose.'

Off the field, Rena is a physiotherapist and a health and wellness coach. In school, she loved sports, and she also loved science – so physiotherapy was a no-brainer! Rena is always very modest and keen to share the glory with those who have supported her: 'To become a successful player, you need support as a person. The players who tend to play for years at a high level tend to get great support from the people around them.'

In 2017, Rena retired from the inter-county game aged 31, and to this day she is one of the most decorated Gaelic sportspeople of all time. Do you think her record of 18 All-Ireland medals will ever be broken?

THE BIG MATCH DAY

THE PLAYERS AND managers are not the only people we need to make the big match day come to life. The fans are a huge part of the culture, and the matches would be nowhere near as exciting without the noise and the colour they bring.

The day of an All-Ireland final at Croke Park is particularly exciting. The face-painted, flag-carrying fans travel from early morning, sandwiches in hand, to the greatest stadium in the land. The commentators take their seats as the Artane Band tune their instruments ahead of the pre-match parade. The stadium stewards and chefs and baristas clock in from early morning, ready to feed the masses, and the turnstiles click nearly 90,000 times before throw-in! The team bus passes down Jones' Road about an hour before throw-in, so you'd better be there early to wish them luck. If you don't have a ticket, you can listen to the radio or watch on TV.

There are so many uniquely Irish elements to the big match day – let's explore a few!

FIELDS IN FOCUS

EVERY COUNTY IN Ireland has a principal stadium or pitch, and some even have two! Croke Park is in Dublin, but the Dubs also have Parnell Park on the northside of the city. Cork has Páirc Uí Chaoimh and Páirc Uí Rinn, while Galway has Tuam Stadium and Pearse Stadium. Having the advantage of playing at home is always considered an asset for an important championship match.

SUPER STADIUMS

The GAA has some of the best stadiums in the world. Croke Park is the biggest and the best, but here's a few more.

NOWLAN PARK
Some global music icons have performed at Nowlan Park, including Dolly Parton, Bruce Springsteen and Bob Dylan, but it's also home to the stars of Kilkenny hurling. It's the principal ground for the Cats and is located on the edge of Kilkenny city. Like most county grounds, the seats are painted in the county colours to match the players' jerseys – in this case, black and amber.

FITZGERALD STADIUM
This is probably one of the most beautiful settings for any stadium anywhere in the world. It's nestled in the picturesque tourist town of Killarney, and from the main stand you can see the rolling hills of the Kerry Mountains in the background. Watching an evening match at Fitzgerald Stadium with the sun setting behind the stands is a real treat. It was named after former footballer Dick Fitzgerald and was opened in 1936.

ST TIERNACH'S PARK
Not only is St Tiernach's Park in Clones the biggest GAA ground in Monaghan, it is also the principal GAA ground for Ulster. Lots of closely fought Ulster finals have been played at Clones, and there is little to rival the atmosphere on a summer's afternoon when the stands and terraces are packed. It holds 36,000 people!

PÁIRC TAILTEANN

Named after the ancient Tailteann Games, this is County Meath's principal ground. It holds 11,000 people and was awarded best playing surface at a county ground by the GAA in 2021.

DID YOU KNOW?

Long before tickets and seating came into GAA grounds, you could jump over a fence or climb onto the roof of a stand and watch a match for free. Those days are long gone now, with official ticketing and turnstiles at every venue. Oh, well.

SEMPLE STADIUM

Tipperary (the Premier County) is known as 'The Home of Hurling', because Thurles is where the GAA was founded. Semple Stadium is the principal ground for Tipperary, but it also stages Munster championship matches and finals. When Semple is full, it can sometimes feel like the ground is shaking, such is the noise and excitement of the fans. Did you know that, apart from the All-Ireland finals, the Munster hurling final is the most watched GAA match on TV every year?

CROKE PARK: THE HISTORY

FROM BUTTERLY FIELD to Jones' Road to Croke Park, GAA HQ has had quite the journey to become what it is today.

This is the map included in the legal agreement between Frank Dineen and the GAA in 1913.

BLOODY SUNDAY

This was one of the darkest days in Irish history. On 21 November 1920, Dublin were playing Tipperary in an All-Ireland final at Croke Park, and there was a brilliant atmosphere among the packed crowd. British soldiers came into the stadium and fired their guns into the crowd as an act of retaliation for the killing earlier in the day of 14 British operatives. Thirteen spectators were killed, including a 10-year-old boy called Jerome O'Leary. Michael Hogan, a footballer from the Tipperary team, was also killed, and to this day the main stand is named in his honour.

BUTTERLY?

In 1864, a man called Maurice Butterly rented land near Clonliffe Road in Drumcondra, Co. Dublin. It became known as 'Butterly's Field' and hosted athletics games like running and jumping. (Some say there were even events like chariot racing!) In 1884, it was sold and became known as Jones' Road. The GAA had to pay rent to stage matches there.

In 1908, Frank Dineen bought the land and held it in trust for the GAA until they could afford to buy it. In 1913, the GAA finally bought Jones' Road, and only then did it get its new name – Croke Memorial Park, or Páirc An Chrócaigh, after Archbishop Croke, one of the GAA's first patrons.

HILL 16

Croke Park has an unusual shape. It's a classic sports bowl most of the way around, except for the Hill 16 end. Did you ever wonder where the Hill – or more accurately 'Dineen Hill 16' – got its name? It used to be just a mound of soil, and supporters who didn't have seats could stand there and enjoy the matches.

In 1936, the soil was replaced with concrete, and the story goes that the rubble was from buildings on O'Connell Street that had been destroyed during the 1916 Easter Rising – hence the name Hill 16. In 2006, the GAA renamed the terrace Dineen Hill 16, in honour of Frank Dineen, the man who first bought the grounds Croke Park is built on. Fans love that Hill 16 is a standing uncovered terrace, so it is unlikely the bowl shape will ever be completed.

A NEW ERA

Between 2007 and 2009, while Lansdowne Road was being redeveloped, the GAA allowed Ireland's rugby and soccer teams to stage their home games at Croke Park. This was a landmark decision, especially considering the history of the Ban (when members of the GAA weren't allowed to watch or take part in sports like rugby and soccer). One of the most remarkable days during that time was 26 February 2007, when England played Ireland in the 6 Nations. Because of Ireland's turbulent history with British rule, and the awful atrocity of Bloody Sunday, this was seen as the dawning of a new era – when the people of modern Ireland welcomed the 'old enemy' to their home ground. Watch videos of that day and hear how loudly the crowd sang 'Amhrán na bhFiann'.

CROKE PARK: BEHIND THE SCENES

CROKE PARK IS the pride of every Gaelic games fan. It's a rare treat to attend a match when there's a packed house – if you're lucky enough to have been there on All-Ireland final day, I'm sure you know just how special it can be!

GANTRY: This is where commentators and broadcasters sit. It's also called the commentary box.

TUNNEL: The passage through which players enter or leave the pitch.

HOGAN STAND: This is where silverware is presented to championship winners – in other words, the place where dreams come true!

SKYLINE: Are you afraid of heights? If you're brave enough to stand 44m above ground, a tour guide will take you to the very top of the stadium, where you can walk along a special walkway on the roof. Don't look down!

FAMOUS VISITORS: In 1972, Muhammad Ali – the greatest boxer of all time – took part in a special bout staged at Croke Park. Pope Francis also visited Croke Park on 25 August 2018. Just like for a match, 80,000 people filled the stadium to get a glimpse of the pontiff.

HILL 16: The Hill 16 big screen is 126m². That's almost 450 times larger than a standard 32-inch TV!

A PACKED HOUSE

It's remarkable to think that a largely amateur organisation in a country as small as Ireland boasts the third largest sports stadium in Europe, but only Wembley Stadium and the Camp Nou are bigger than our very own Croke Park! (The Bernabéu in Madrid is being renovated and its capacity will pip GAA HQ by a couple of thousand when completed!)

STADIUM	CAPACITY
Camp Nou	99,354
Wembley	90,000
Croke Park	82,300

PITCH: The field of play. The Spire (127m high) could fit comfortably on the Croke Park pitch (144m long) and any other football, hurling and camogie pitch.

GAA MUSEUM: The GAA Museum houses many important artefacts, including a rulebook from the Hurling Federation of Argentina.

TURNSTILES: This is where fans enter the stadium after showing their ticket.

STANDS: There are the Hogan, Nally, Cusack and Davin stands, as well as Dineen Hill 16. If you lined up all 70,000 seats in Croke Park in one continuous line, they would stretch the length of the Dublin City Marathon route!

PARADES AND PAGEANTRY

THERE IS A special series of events that must take place on the day of a big match. The GAA produce match programmes with the timetable, which is known as 'Clár an Lae'. These events – the parades and pageantry – are especially significant on the day of an All-Ireland final.

PRE-MATCH PARADE

The pre-match parade is a distinctly Irish tradition – and it really only happens for Gaelic games. The two starting teams, numbers 1 to 15, line up behind their captain and parade around the pitch to be applauded by their fans. The cheering fans wish them luck and make as much noise as they can as the players pass. The teams usually follow a band around the field – this could be a local band or, in the case of the All-Ireland final, the Artane Band.

BANNA ARD AIDHIN

The Artane Band has been around for more than a hundred years, and it's played for US presidents and British royalty. It first played at a GAA match in 1886! The band was originally set up for young musicians who attended the Artane Industrial School. It was for boys only and was known as the Artane Boys' Band until 2004, when girls were allowed to join. The school closed in 1969, but the band remains a core element of All-Ireland final day.

MEETING THE PRESIDENT

For the big games at Croke Park, the president of Ireland and the taoiseach arrive to a hullabaloo. The president will have a garda escort and sometimes even bodyguards! Have you ever seen the president's car being followed into the Croke Park tunnels by police motorbikes? It's quite the spectacle. On All-Ireland final day, a red carpet is rolled out onto the pitch for the president to walk on as they greet the teams. The president will shake hands with every player and wish them luck.

AMHRÁN NA BHFIANN

The national anthem, 'Amhrán na bhFiann', is played before most big matches, but is especially significant on All-Ireland final day. Sometimes a famous singer will do the honours – though it's not like the NFL where superstars like Beyoncé and Lady Gaga sing 'The Star-Spangled Banner'!

THROW-IN

And, finally, the most anticipated event: THROW-IN! Did you know the ball used to be thrown in by a member of the clergy? There are old black-and-white photos of bishops standing facing the crowd and throwing the ball over their head into the fray behind them. Nowadays, the referee gathers the four midfielders in the centre of the field and, if it's Gaelic football, throws the ball into the air or, if it's hurling, tosses the sliotar between them on the ground. Let the games begin!

FUN FACT

Kilkenny paraded with 16 players on the day of the 1957 All-Ireland final. The 16th man was an English actor named John Gregson. He was playing the part of an Irish binman whose hurling team made it to an All-Ireland final. The movie company paid both teams and the GAA to allow them to film the match-day parade, and Gregson marched along in a Kilkenny jersey.

MATCH DAY

WHEN YOU GO to a match on a Sunday afternoon, you might sit in the stands or head for the terraces. Do you bring pocket money for snacks? Maybe you have a long drive up to Croke Park and bring a packed lunch. Everybody's match day is different – but what does it look like behind the scenes?

BEHIND THE SCENES

Next time you're lucky enough to be at Croke Park on a big match day, take a minute at half-time to notice all the people busily at work. Can you see the radio commentators up high in the Hogan Stand? Is there an ambulance down at the Nally Stand gate? Do you see the sideline reporter hanging around near the tunnel, looking for clues about what subs will come on in the second half?

LIGHTS UP

The first person to arrive on a big match day is the stadium director. They effectively 'turn on the lights' and make sure the venue is ready for all the people who will work at Croke Park that day.

READ ALL ABOUT IT

There are hundreds of media personnel in Croke Park on a big match day. The TV camera crews arrive super early because they have to set up their cameras and all the cables before anybody else is there to get in the way!

TOP TIP

The best way to be involved on a big match day is to volunteer as a steward. They are usually near the ticket booths or guarding the pitch from possible 'invaders'. They don't get paid, but they don't have to buy a ticket and they get good and close to the action!

THE TEAMS

The teams usually arrive by bus about an hour before throw-in, and very often they've spent some time at a nearby pitch for a warm-up. You'll spot the team bus because it usually has a sign in the window saying something like 'TYRONE SENIOR FOOTBALL TEAM'. Any fans in nearby cars will beep in excitement! The bus drives under the stands and the players go straight to the dressing rooms.

THE WARM-UP

The players' match-day jerseys are there waiting for them, usually set up hours in advance by their kit managers. There is a special warm-up room attached to the main dressing rooms in Croke Park. It has an AstroTurf surface and is big enough to have a puck around to settle those match-day nerves!

CAREFUL NOW

Every inter-county team has a physio and a doctor with them on a big match day. If a player gets injured, these people are allowed to run onto the field to check if the player is OK. If a player is badly injured, the medics may have to carry them off the field on a stretcher and bring them to the nearest hospital.

GRUB'S UP

82,300 mouths is a lot to feed … and then there are all those hard-working stewards and medics and journalists who need a cup of tea too! No matter what you feel like having, you'll find it at Croke Park. There are 56 cafes, 9 restaurants and 22 bars.

THE FANS

GAELIC GAMES FANS share a strong sense of identity – they feel they are part of a tribe. No matter where you travel around the world, you will always spot an Irish person wearing their county jersey.

THE BUILD-UP

Big GAA matches traditionally took place on Sunday afternoons – and most still do. Groups of families and friends would pile into their cars and set off early, often after attending Sunday-morning mass together. They'd arrive at the grounds early, get a good parking spot and gather around the open boot of the car to eat a packed lunch. That was the big match day off to a great start!

THE ULTRAS

Sometimes fans travel in large packs, gather on the terraces and bring a *lot* of noise and colour to the big match day. These energetic groups of fans are known as Ultras, and you'll see examples in lots of different sports. The GAA Ultras are all about fun. They paint their faces, sing songs and sometimes bang drums or let off flares. They often parade through the town on their way to the ground. Two well-known groups of Ultras are Cuala GAA in Dublin and Austin Stacks in Tralee.

SUPERFANS

A well-known Kilkenny fan often dresses up as Elvis!

This Cork fan wears a huge sombrero to every Cork match

THE TUNES!

One unique pre-match build-up for a big game – especially if there's been a drought of success in the county – is for a local band to write a song about their great team. One famous example is a song about the Kerry footballers in 1982. It was released before the All-Ireland final and included lyrics like 'it's hard to believe we've won the five-in-a-row'. Kerry were expected to beat Offaly, but a late goal by Séamus Darby made sure they didn't – so proceed with caution if you're putting pen to paper!

PITCH INVASIONS

Have you ever heard older people talk about the 'good old days'? Well, sometimes they're right … It used to be a lot of fun at the final whistle of an exciting All-Ireland. The *second* the referee blew the final whistle, hundreds of people would stream onto the pitch, their flags flying in the air behind them as they ran. People would swarm around the winning players and manager and lift them into the air, chanting their names and singing songs about them. But pitch invasions are not allowed at All-Ireland finals any more. This is to prevent people getting injured in the crowd and also to protect the grass pitches.

FUN FACT

The Offaly hurling fans staged a sit-down protest on the pitch in Croke Park when the referee blew the final whistle two minutes too early in the 1998 All-Ireland semi-final! They refused to leave the pitch until a replay was ordered, and they got their wish! Not only did Offaly beat Clare, they even beat Kilkenny in the final. All thanks to the passionate Faithful fans!

THE LINGO

AH REF!

EVERY SPORT HAS its own special lingo. You'll hear it on the radio or at your local pitch. To the uninitiated, it can sound like a different language … 'There was a bit of a shemozzle at the edge of the parallelogram, and the ref sent a few to the line.' So here's the ultimate guide to what to say on match day. Learn this lingo to speak like a pro and blend in with the crowd.

DICTIONARY

Here are the most common words and phrases – and a few fun ones thrown in for good measure!

DIRTY BALL: The ball can be spotlessly clean, but if you can win 'dirty ball' you're a credit to your team. It just means you will move mountains to get a 50/50 ball.

DUMMY TEAM: When a manager doesn't want the opposition (or anyone else!) to know who's starting in a match, they will release a fake ('dummy') team to the county board and media.

HAMES: An absolute mess. You can make a 'hames' of a pass or a ball – it's a frustrated insult!

MELEE OR FRACAS: The most serious version of a fight on the pitch, a melee or a fracas could be described as absolute chaos, and sometimes includes violence. The referee usually needs to get his red card out after a melee.

OFF THE BALL: Anything that happens when the ball is not in play, or that happens away from where the ball is in play. It could be fisticuffs between the full back and full forward of opposing teams while the ball is sailing over the bar at the other end of the field!

SHEMOZZLE: The greatest description of an argument between opposing teams, a shemozzle will usually involve at least three players, and the ref usually has to stop the play to calm things down.

THE SQUARE (which isn't a square!): There are two rectangles in the goal mouth – nobody knows why they're known officially as 'parallelograms'. The small rectangle is referred to as 'the square', even though it's not a square in shape.

TOP O' THE RIGHT: A position on the field – right corner forward!

HAMES!

WHAT'S IN A NAME?

The GAA has some of the best nicknames. For the most part they make *no* sense whatsoever, and yet they seem to stick! Did you know there are a ton of famous Michaels in the game? There's Michael 'Babs' Keating and Michael 'Hopper' McGrath, Michael 'Ducksie' Walsh and Michael 'Brick' Walsh – and Micky 'Spike' Fagan, of course! Have you heard of The Rock, Pebbles, Gooch and Banty?

THE ROCK – AND PEBBLES!

At the height of his hurling prowess in the mid-2000s, you'd never get past the Cork full-back Diarmuid 'The Rock' O'Sullivan. In keeping with the theme, his younger brother Paudie became known as 'Pebbles'.

GOOCH

One of the greatest footballers to ever grace a pitch was Colm Cooper from Kerry. He was first called 'Gooch' by a teammate in Dr Crokes club, Peter O'Brien. As a child, Peter thought Colm looked like a doll he'd seen with bright red hair, and the doll's name was 'The Gooch'!

BANTY

Séamus 'Banty' McEnaney is a football manager and former player from Monaghan, and he even called his first pub Banty's Bar. It turns out his dad gave him the nickname as a child. Séamus had two prominent bones in his chest, and his dad said he looked like a 'banty hen' (a bantam). The name stuck!

THE MEDIA

CROKE PARK HOLDS a lot of people (82,300 to be exact), but more than a MILLION people tune in to watch All-Ireland finals on TV! How do you stay tuned on match day? Do you watch your county on TV, listen to commentary on the radio or track the scores on social media?

HOT OFF THE PRESS

All the principal GAA grounds have a special area high up in the stands known as 'the gantry'. Next time you're at a match, look up and see if you can spot it. You'll see the TV cameras perched up there with the match commentators. Some journalists even bring binoculars, in case an incident happens too far away and they can't make out the player's jersey number.

BREAKING NEWS!

Would you like to report on the action? What job do you think you'd like?

PRESENTER: the person in the TV or radio studio who anchors the pre- and post-match discussions.

REPORTER: the person who interviews the players and managers before and after the game.

PRINT JOURNALIST: the person who goes to the matches, sits in the press box and writes match reports or special features about players. They can write for newspapers, magazines or online websites.

COMMENTATOR: the person who sits in the gantry with a special microphone called a 'lip ribbon' and describes the match for the people listening or watching.

TV DIRECTOR: this person sits in a big truck outside the stadium and presses buttons to make sure the TV is showing the right camera shots at the right time.

HAVE YOU HEARD?

Social media means we can watch matches, or even just snippets of goals and incidents, on computers, tablets and smartphones – anywhere, anytime. But imagine having to wait hours after an All-Ireland final finished for your friend or your neighbour to travel home from the match and tell you the final score. It's hard to imagine, but what did people do in the past?

THE WIRELESS

Before the dawn of TV, the plain old radio had a special place in people's hearts. The first radio was called the 'wireless' – because there were no wires linking it to the radio station. Not everyone had a radio, because they were very new – and very expensive. Anyone who owned a radio would invite friends over to share in the experience of listening to the match commentary – they'd even leave the windows open so people could gather outside and follow the action with their ears cocked!

THE BOX

The television was invented in 1927, but very few people had TVs in Ireland until the 1960s. The first Irish TV station was set up in 1961. RTÉ was the only place you could watch Gaelic games. The first TV sets looked like big boxes, with a curved grey screen at the front … and there was no colour. Everything you saw on TV back then was black and white. Imagine trying to follow a match between Cork and Galway if you couldn't see the colours of the red and maroon jerseys!

DID YOU KNOW?

The GAA have their own media platform called GAAGO. It's an app that allows you to access matches on your phone or or your laptop. Imagine telling the people gathered around the wireless in the 1950s about all the ways you enjoy Gaelic games these days.

THE SILVERWARE

THERE'S SOMETHING VERY special about a trophy. It's a mark of success, and a reward for all the hard work and sacrifice it's taken to get to the pinnacle of your sport. The silverware in Gaelic games has an added layer of magic, perhaps because you don't get paid for winning – pride of the parish is prize enough!

THE BIG FOUR

There are four principal cups in Gaelic games. These are awarded to the All-Ireland senior champions in hurling, football, camogie and ladies' football. If you manage to get your hands on one of these, you've made it. Every player has seen their heroes climb the steps of the Hogan Stand and wished to do the same one day.

LIAM MACCARTHY CUP

The Liam MacCarthy Cup is awarded to the winners of the annual All-Ireland Senior Hurling Championship. This cup is very distinctive – its design is based on a medieval drinking vessel. It is named after Liam MacCarthy, who was born in London to Cork parents and grew up speaking Irish and playing hurling. He commissioned the cup and donated it to Central Council at Croke Park. It was first awarded in 1923, to Limerick.

SAM MAGUIRE CUP

The Sam Maguire Cup is awarded to the winners of the annual All-Ireland Senior Football Championship and was first awarded to Kildare in 1928. It is named after Sam Maguire, who, coincidentally, served on the London GAA county board alongside Liam MacCarthy. Maguire was born in Cork, but emigrated to London for work, and played with the London Hibernians Gaelic football team. After he died, his friends raised funds to commission a cup in his memory and donated it to Croke Park.

O'DUFFY CUP

The winners of the All-Ireland Senior Camogie Championship are awarded the O'Duffy Cup. It's named after Seán O'Duffy, who was a member of Kilmacud Crokes GAA Club in Dublin. He presented the trophy to the Camogie Association in 1932.

BRENDAN MARTIN CUP

The All-Ireland Senior Ladies' Football Championship is one of the most difficult cups to win, because there are so many teams in ladies' football, and the sport is very competitive. The Brendan Martin Cup is named after a native of Tullamore in Offaly, who was one of the first administrators of the newly founded Ladies Gaelic Football Association in the 1970s. Brendan Martin bought the cup himself in 1974 and donated it to the LGFA.

NEXT BEST THING...

Only the very best teams can win a cup like the Liam MacCarthy – that cup is the holy grail of hurling!

Not every team can even enter the Liam MacCarthy competition, as they simply aren't strong enough contenders. So there are lower-tier cups for divisions below the senior football and hurling championships.

The Tailteann Cup is a competition for lower-tier inter-county football sides, while hurling has *five* different cup competitions based on ranking, so there are far more opportunities to claim silverware in senior inter-county hurling than football:

2ND TIER
Joe McDonagh Cup

3RD TIER
Christy Ring Cup

4TH TIER
Nicky Rackard Cup

5TH TIER
Lory Meagher Cup

DID YOU KNOW?

None of the four original senior cups is still being presented. The original Liam MacCarthy Cup is now on display in the GAA Museum, and the cup that is handed out is a replica.

SPOTLIGHT ON: MÍCHEÁL Ó MUIRCHEARTAIGH

THE PEOPLE WHO bring Gaelic games to life for those who can't be there are a huge part of match day. When Mícheál Ó Muircheartaigh started commentating on Gaelic games, there was no such thing as television. He began his career working on 'the wireless' – an old-fashioned name for a radio – and that's where he was at his best. He commentated for six decades on RTÉ Radio 1, which was for a long time the only radio station on which you could hear Gaelic match commentaries.

Mícheál is a Kerryman, from a place called Dún Síon, and he is a native Irish speaker. Tá blas gleoite aige agus é ag labhairt as Gaeilge agus is minic a bhíodh frásaí as Gaeilge fite fuaite ina chuid tráchtaireachtaí as Béarla. That means, 'He has a lovely *blas* when he's speaking Irish and he would often weave Irish phrases into his English commentaries.' (The word *blas* literally means 'taste', but when used about the spoken Irish language it means how natural a speaker someone is.) In fact, when Mícheál began his career way back in 1949, he used to commentate exclusively *as Gaeilge* for the minor matches. To this day, the GAA insist that the commentary for minor All-Ireland finals is in Irish.

Mícheál's last ever commentary was on the International Rules game between Ireland and Australia in 2010. His last All-Ireland was earlier that autumn – the football final between Cork and Down on 19 September 2010. Years later, Mícheál was awarded the only All-Star award of 2020. No player received an award that year, due to the Covid-19 pandemic.

Mícheál's retirement signalled the end of an era. He had taken over from the legendary game-caller Michael O'Hehir, and now it was time to pass on the baton once again. Both men had worked in an era with little access to media, and no social media, so their roles as commentators were sacred. If they didn't commentate, no one would know what was happening at Croke Park or the Hyde!

WHOSE LINE IS IT?

Known for his poetic turns of phrase, Mícheál's radio commentary was always engaging, and he painted vivid pictures of the action. Here are some of his best lines.

'SEÁN ÓG Ó HAILPÍN: HIS FATHER'S FROM FERMANAGH, HIS MOTHER'S FROM FIJI – NEITHER A HURLING STRONGHOLD.'

'THE STOPWATCH HAS STOPPED. IT'S UP TO GOD AND THE REFEREE NOW. THE REFEREE IS PAT HORAN. GOD IS GOD.'

'TEDDY LOOKS AT THE BALL, THE BALL LOOKS AT TEDDY.'

'PAT FOX HAS IT ON HIS HURL AND IS MOTORING WELL NOW, BUT HERE COMES JOE RABBITTE HOT ON HIS TAIL … I'VE SEEN IT ALL NOW, A RABBITTE CHASING A FOX AROUND CROKE PARK!'

'ANTHONY LYNCH, THE CORK CORNER BACK, WILL BE THE LAST PERSON TO LET YOU DOWN – HIS PEOPLE ARE UNDERTAKERS.'

'HE GRABS THE SLIOTAR. HE'S ON THE 50! HE'S ON THE 40! HE'S ON THE 30 … HE'S ON THE GROUND!'

DID YOU KNOW?

Mícheál is the main commentator on the PlayStation 2 game *Gaelic Games: Football*.

CALLING ALL GAELS!

GAELIC GAMES ARE now considered global sports, and Gaelic culture is thriving off the back of them. Have you noticed how so many of the competitions have names *as Gaeilge*? The link between the Irish language and our national sports is very strong, and we already know it goes right back to when the founders of the GAA wanted to protect the national culture, language and sports of Ireland.

When you grow up and travel the world, don't forget to pack your hurl! There are hurling and football teams in all corners of the world, with thriving communities of Gaels just waiting to welcome new teammates. No matter what age you are or which country you hail from, you'll find a home and a team for you. There really is something for everyone in the great world of Gaelic games.

GAA AROUND THE WORLD

HAVE YOU HEARD of the Jakarta Dragonflies, the Fog City Harps or the Daegu Fianna? These are GAA clubs located thousands of miles from Croke Park. There are thriving GAA communities all around the world. In fact, one in every five GAA clubs is located outside Ireland – New York alone has 23!

A HOME AWAY FROM HOME

During the 19th and 20th centuries, many people were forced to leave Ireland in search of work. They set up GAA clubs in their new communities to try to make themselves feel at home. Over the years, these clubs have become social hubs for the Irish abroad. They bring people together and help create a home away from home.

NEW YORK STATE OF MIND

In 1926, the GAA bought Gaelic Park in New York. It was a place for Irish immigrants in the Bronx to meet up and play hurling. To this day, it's home to a big community of Irish people and the descendants of Irish immigrants, and it's also where the New York inter-county team plays its home games. Clubs in the USA take part in divisional championships, a bit like the Ulster or Connacht championships, and then qualify for national finals.

DID YOU KNOW?

In 2021, for the first time ever, a New York county board delegate was elected president of the GAA! Originally from Bishopstown, County Cork, Larry McCarthy lives in the USA and is a member of the Sligo Football Club in New York.

GOING GLOBAL

These days, young people who move abroad in search of adventure line out for clubs in places as varied as Boston and Melbourne, Kuala Lumpur and Delhi. The most northerly GAA club in the world is the Oulu Elks – their grounds are only 160km from the Arctic Circle! The South African Gaels are the first GAA club in the world to field a team without a single Irish player. They were founded in 2010 and have taken part in several GAA World Games. The GAA World Games is one of the biggest global events and has been held four times since 2015. The 2023 event took place over five days, in Derry. Two thousand players from 100 teams around the world took part.

FANTASTIC FACTS

A NEW ERA

The London inter-county team has been around so long that there are English-born players lining out in the All-Ireland championships. When the GAA was founded, it would have been unheard of for an English person, with an English accent, to play hurling or Gaelic football.

HURLOWEEN

Have you ever heard of Hurloween? It's a new craze that's been taking North America by storm. GAA teams dress up in Halloween costumes and stage hurling matches and events. The idea originated in Milwaukee Hurling Club in Wisconsin.

THE DUBAI 7S

Between 2007 and 2014, the Dubai Celts hosted a hugely popular international competition for the 7s version of hurling. Some of the competing clubs came from the United Arab Emirates, Bahrain, Oman, Qatar, South Africa and Singapore, and were joined by visiting teams from Ireland and across Europe. It was a busy one-day event – up to 100 matches would take place in one venue!

AN GHAEILGE AGUS AN CULTÚR

REMEMBER HOW GAELIC games were banned by British kings? Well, it wasn't just the games they tried to suppress, but the language and the culture too. When Michael Cusack and his compatriots set up the GAA in 1884, they made provisions to protect Gaelic culture, as well as Gaelic sports. This promise was even written into the rulebook!

RULE 4 OF THE GAA: 'The Association shall actively support the Irish language, traditional Irish dancing, music, song and other aspects of Irish culture. It shall foster an awareness and love of the national ideals in the people of Ireland, and assist in promoting a community spirit through its clubs.'

AN GHAEILGE

When you think about the names of various competitions held by the GAA, the link between Gaelic games and the Irish language is obvious: *scór* is the Irish word for a music score, and *féile* means festival. The GAA president is always referred to as Uachtarán Chumann Lúthcleas Gael. Also, have you noticed how, when an All-Ireland Cup is presented, the captain always begins their speech in Irish: 'Tá an-áthas orm an corn seo a ghlacadh, ar son …'?

Here are some simple phrases *as Gaeilge* you can use on and off the pitch!

TARRAING AIR — Pull on it

MARCÁIL SUAS! — Mark up!

THAR AN TRASNÁN — Over the bar

BEIR BUA — Good luck!

AMACH AR AN GCLIATHÁN — Out on the wing

BHFUIL SIBH RÉIDH? — Are you ready?

CAITH ISTEACH AN LIATHRÓID — Throw in the ball

MAITH THÚ! — Well done!

CEATHARLACH ABÚ! — Up Carlow!

CÚILÍN! — Point!

CÚL! — Goal!

SCÓÓÓR!

Did you know that an entire division of the GAA is dedicated to promoting Irish culture? It's called Scór, and every year it organises big competitions in things like Irish music, dance and drama, for children and adults. It was set up in 1969 by a man called Derry Gowen from Fermoy, County Cork. Derry wanted the tribal element of rivalry that exists between GAA clubs to extend beyond the sports fields and into the traditional Irish pastimes of music and dance. It was also a way for people to represent their GAA clubs in the winter when hurling and football took a break!

Scór is divided into two age levels, Scór na nÓg, for young people, and Scór Sinsir, for those over 17. Some counties even host Scór na bPáistí for primary school children. The competitions have different rounds, so if you win your club competition, you can go on to the county final, and then into the provincial and All-Ireland championships. Just like in hurling and football, All-Ireland Scór champions are presented with their medals by the president of the GAA.

SCÓR EVENTS

RINCE FOIRNE
(céilí dancing)

AMHRÁNAÍOCHT AONAIR
(solo singing)

CEOL UIRLISE
(instrumental music)

SCÉALAÍOCHT
(storytelling)

BAILÉAD GHRÚPA
(ballad group)

NUACHLEAS
(novelty act)

RINCE SEIT
(set dancing)

TRÁTH NA GCEIST
(question time)

CÚL KIDS!

THE REASON GAELIC games have survived for hundreds of years is because the games and the skills have been handed down from generation to generation. Kids like you are the future and probably the most important players in the world of Gaelic games!

NEVER TOO YOUNG …

Were you a member of your club's academy? Well, then you'll know that most of the clubs around Ireland, and even some outside Ireland, have a nursery or academy. Academy coaches are usually parents who get together at the weekend to teach the fundamental skills to their children under seven. The academies show just how important volunteering is to the GAA. Nobody gets paid – everybody is there simply to make sure that the native sports of Ireland survive and thrive! Lots of clubs will hold a graduation after kids reach the age of seven. Medals and certificates are often awarded, and the next big step is Go Games!

GO GAMES

Things get very exciting as an under 8 in the world of Gaelic games. For the first time, the county board organises official matches against other clubs, and you begin to feel that tribal culture of the GAA. Unlike the adult game, a goal in Go Games is worth one point, while a traditional point (over the bar) is worth three. But the best part? It's called Go Games because *everybody* gets a go! There are no substitutes and no such thing as an A team or a B team. This doesn't happen until under 12s.

CÚL CAMPS

Every summer, more than 140,000 children aged 6–13 take part in the GAA's Cúl Camps. The best thing is the gear. Every child who registers for a GAA Cúl Camp receives a set of playing gear and a rucksack. I bet you've seen lots of Cúl Camp jerseys and jumpers around the country and even on your holidays abroad!

FLASHY FÉILE

Ask any famous player from the last few decades about their most treasured memories in Gaelic games, and I bet some will tell you about Féile. Féile na nGael and Féile Peil na nÓg are the All-Ireland club festivals for hurling, football, camogie, rounders and handball for under 15s.

At 14 and 15 years of age, Féile weekend competitions are a huge part of the lives of young players. For many, it's the first time they travel far away, overnight, to play for their club. There is a huge sense of pride in winning Féile, and it whets the appetite for many young players who go on to play and win All-Irelands at senior level.

MOL AN ÓIGE

Have you ever tried out the Skills Challenges set by the GAA? There are lots of videos on the GAA website where senior inter-county stars demonstrate skills like hand pass, toe tap, high catch and jab lift. Give it a go and challenge yourself to improve!

DON'T FORGET YOUR GUMSHIELD!

DID YOU KNOW?

During the Covid-19 pandemic, most players couldn't train with their team. Well, instead a virtual challenge was set up to test soloing skills. Maybe you took part. Did you upload your video online?

ACKNOWLEDGEMENTS

EVANNE NÍ CHUILINN

Writing this book (my first!) was a steep learning curve for me, and I feel so lucky to have had the opportunity to work with such talented publishers and editors at Gill, and, of course, illustrator extraordinaire Donough O'Malley. The greatest 'thank you' goes to my family, though. I took on this project just as we became a family of five and had never been more stretched. Thanks to Brian and the kids for their gifts of time and patience, and for always being my biggest hype squad.

DONOUGH O'MALLEY

A massive 'thank you' to everyone at Gill and to Evanne for having me take part in such an amazing project. To Liz and Graham for their design skills and patience. To my wife, Emily, for putting up with all the early mornings and late nights. And finally to my dad, who was a dedicated Mayo fan all his life, and to RB, who loved a small ball.

INDEX

A

All-Ireland Final Day 11, 63
    official throw-in 71
    parades and pageantry 70–71
Alonso, Xabi 44
Amhrán na bhFiann (Irish national anthem) 71
Antrim ('The Saffrons') 15
Armagh, Gaelic football 46, 47, 53
Artane Band 70–71
Athenry GFC (County Galway) 29
Aussie Rules football 49, 51, 57–58
Australian Football League (AFL) 43, 58
    see also Aussie Rules football; International Rules

B

Ballyhale Shamrocks GFC (County Kilkenny) 29, 40
Birr GFC (County Offaly) 29
Blackrock GFC (County Cork) 29
Boylan, Seán 52
Brady, Paul 'The Gunner' 37, 38
Brendan Martin Cup (Ladies' Gaelic football) 43, 81
British rule 9, 11, 18
Browne, Declan 51
Broy, Ned 13
Buckley, Rena 60–61
Butterly, Maurice 66

C

camogie 11, 12, 21, 24–25
    rules 25
Canavan, Peter 50
Carey, D.J. 36, 37, 40
Carlow ('The Scallion Eaters') 15
Carron (County Clare) 18
Cavan ('The Breffni County') 15
    Gaelic football 46
Christy Ring Cup 81
Clare ('The Banner') 15, 74
    hurling 29, 33
Clifford, David 51
Cluxton, Stephen 51
Cody, Brian 29, 32, 41
Connolly, Joe 29
Cooney, Joe 29
Cooper, Colm 'Gooch' 77
Cork ('The Rebels') 15, 17
    Gaelic football 47, 50, 53
    hurling 28, 29, 32
Corkery, Briege 61
County boards 11, 14
    county colours 16–17
    county nicknames 15
Croke Park (Dublin) 11, 19, 28, 64
    Bloody Sunday (1920) 66, 67
    Hill 16 67, 69
    history 66–67
    see also All-Ireland Final Day; Cusack Stand; Davin Stand; Dineen Hill 16; Hogan Stand
Croke, Archbishop Thomas 10
Cúl Kids (club academy system) 90–91
Cummins, Brendan 35
Cusack, Bridget 18
Cusack, Margaret (née Woods) 18
Cusack, Matthew 18
Cusack, Michael 10, 18–19, 21
Cusack Stand (Croke Park) 10, 13, 19, 69

D

Daly, Anthony 33
Darby, Séamus 47
Davin, Maurice 10
Davin Stand (Croke Park) 69
Davitt, Michael 10
Derry, Gaelic football 46, 47
Dineen, Frank 66, 67
Dineen Hill 16 67, 69
Donegal, Gaelic football 47, 51
Down 17
    Gaelic football 46, 47
Downey, Angela 30
Downey, Ann 30
Doyle, Jimmy 28
dual code players 51, 60–61
Dublin ('The Jackeens') 15
    Gaelic football 46, 47, 52

E

Earley, Dermot, Sr 51

F

Fagan, Micky 'Spike' 77
fans 74–75, 76–77
    GAA lingo 76–77
Farrell, Cyril 33
Féile na nGael 91
Féile Peil na nÓg 91
Fitzgerald, Davy 22, 33
Fitzgerald, Dick 64
Fitzgerald Stadium (Kerry) 64
'foreign' sports ban 11, 67

G

GAA lingo
    'dirty ball' 76
    'dummy team' 76
    'hames' 76
    'melee/fracas' 76
    'off the ball' 76
    player nicknames 77
    'shemozzle' 76
    'the square' 76
    'top o' the right' 76
Gaelic Athletic Association (GAA) 7, 10–11, 12, 18, 43
    club and county structure 14–15
    county stadiums and pitches 64–65
    global presence 85–87
    governance 14
    Irish language and culture promotion 7, 11, 85, 88–89
    promotion of Gaelic games by diaspora 85–86
    Rule 21 11
    Rule 27 11
    Rule 42 11
    see also Cúl Kids; Scór

Gaelic football 8–9, 43–55
    bainisteoirí 54–55
    county winning trends 46–47
        1940s 46
        1950s 46
        1960s 46
        1970s 46
        1980s 47
        1990s 47
        2000s 47
        2010s 47
        2020s 47
    famous county rivalries 52–53
    notable players 50–51
    positions 44
    skills 45
    crouch pick-up 45
    handpass 45
    high catch 45
    hook kick 45
    punt kick 45
    solo 45
Gaelic games
    origins 8–9, 11, 18–19
        see also camogie; Gaelic football; hurling; rounders
Gaelic League 18
Gaelic Park (New York) 86
Gaelic4Mothers&Others 49
Gaelic4Teens 49
Galway ('The Tribesmen')
    Gaelic football
        46, 47, 53, 54
    hurling 29, 33
Gavin, Jim 47
Gowen, Derry 89
Gregson, John 71
Griffin, Liam 32

H

handball 11, 13, 21, 36–37
    ball alley 27, 36
    softball and hardball 37
    wall ball 27
Harte, Mickey 50, 55
Heffernan, Kevin 'Heffo'
    46, 52, 55
Hegarty, Gearóid 31
Hodgers, Oliver 34
Hogan, Michael 66

Hogan Stand (Croke Park)
    68, 80
Hughes, Eugene 'Nudie' 51
hurling 7, 21–41
    clubs 29
    high fielding 23
    hurl(ey) 26
        bas 26
        heel 26
        toe 26
    hurling 7s 23
    managers 32–33
    players 30–31
    rules 25
    skills
        jab lift 23, 26
        puck-outs 23
        solo 23
        strike from the hand 23
        sliotar 27
    teams 28–29

I

'International Rules' 43, 58–59

J

Jackman, Patricia 35
James Stephens GFC 29
Joe McDonagh Cup 81

K

Keating, Michael 'Babs' 33, 77
Keegan, Lee 51
Keher, Eddie 30
Kelly, Eoin 31
Kennelly, Tadhg 57
Kerry ('The Kingdom') 15, 17
    Gaelic football 46, 47, 50, 52, 53
Kiely, John 29, 31, 33
Kildare ('The Lilywhites') 17
    Gaelic football 47
Kilkenny ('The Cats') 15
    hurling 28, 29, 32, 71
Kilmacud Crokes GFC 23, 81

L

Ladies Gaelic Football Association
    (LGFA) 12, 48–49
Laois, Gaelic football 50
Leitrim, Gaelic football 54
Liam MacCarthy Cup (hurling)
    21, 22, 32, 80–81
Limerick ('The Treatymen') 15, 31
    hurling 28, 29, 33
Listowel Emmets GFC (County Kerry)
    57
Lory Meagher Cup 81
Loughnane, Ger 29, 33
Louth, Gaelic football 56
Lucan Sarsfields GFC 14

M

Mac Seáin, An tAthair Pól 34
McCarthy, Justin 33
McCarthy, Larry 86
McCarthy, Teddy 'Mac' 50, 60
McCarthy, Thomas St George 10
McEnaney, Séamus 'Banty' 77
McGrath, Ken 31
McGrath, Michael 'Hopper' 77
McKay, John 10
Match Day 72–73
Mayo, Gaelic football 46, 47, 51, 53, 54
Meath ('The Royals') 15
    Gaelic football 47, 52
media 78–79
    gantry 78
    Gaelic football 51
Morgan, Billy 50, 54
Murphy, Michael 51

N

Nally, Pat 19
Nally Stand (Croke Park) 69
National Athletic Sports 19
National Museum (Castlebar) 8
nicknames
    county 15
    players 77
Nicky Rackard Cup 81
Nowlan Park (Kilkenny) 64

O

Ó Muircheartaigh, Mícheál 82–83
O'Brien, Peter 77
O'Connor, Gemma 30, 31
O'Connor, Mark 57
O'Duffy Cup (camogie) 21, 81
O'Duffy, Eoin 13
O'Duffy, Seán 81
O'Dwyer, Mick 52, 54
O'Dwyer, Orla 57
Offaly 74
    Gaelic football 46, 47
    hurling 29
O'Grady, Donal 32
O'Hehir, Mícheál 82
O'Leary, Jerome 66
O'Mahony, John 53, 54
O'Sullivan, Diarmuid 'The Rock' 77
O'Sullivan, Paudie 'Pebbles' 77

P

Páirc Tailteann (Meath) 65
Páirc Úi Chaoimh (Cork) 64
Páirc Úi Rinn (Cork) 64
Parnell, Charles Stewart 10
Parnell Park (Dublin) 64
Pearse Stadium (Galway) 64
Poc Fada competition 34–35
Portnumna GFC (County Galway) 29
Power, John Wyse 10
Provincial Championship 14
'purple patch' 29, 47

R

Rackard, Billy 28, 30
Rackard, Bobby 28, 30
Rackard, Nicky 28, 30
Ramsbottom, Sue 50
Reade, Michael 37
Reilly, Aisling 37
Ring, Christy 28, 29, 30
rounders 11, 13, 21, 38–39
Ryan, Éamonn 60

S

St Tiernach's Park (Monaghan) 64
Sam Maguire Cup (Gaelic football) 43, 46, 80
Scór (music, dance and drama) 89
Semple Stadium (Tipperary) 65
Shannon, Fiona 37
Shannon, Sibéal 37
Sheedy, Liam 33
Shefflin, Henry 28, 30, 40–41
Skills Challenges 91
Sligo 17
Society for the Preservation of the Irish Language 18
Spillane, Pat 51, 53
Stack, Bríd 61
Staunton, Cora 50, 51
Stynes, Jim 57
synthetic hurleys 26

T

Tailteann Cup 8, 81
terminology see GAA lingo
Tipperary ('The Premier County') 15, 17, 33
    Gaelic football 51
    hurling 28, 35
Torpey, Seán 27
Tuam Stadium (Galway) 64
Tuohy, Zach 57
Tyrone, Gaelic football 47, 50, 53, 55

U

United Irishman 11

W

Walsh, Angela 61
Walsh, Michael 'Brick' 77
Walsh, Michael 'Ducksie' 37, 77
Waterford ('The Déise'), hurling 15, 33, 35
Wexford ('The Yellowbellies') 15
    hurling 28, 32

Gill Books

Hume Avenue

Park West

Dublin 12

www.gillbooks.ie

Gill Books is an imprint of M.H. Gill and Co.

Text © Evanne Ní Chuilinn 2023

Illustrations © Donough O'Malley 2023

9780717197569

Design origination by
www.grahamthew.com

Designed by
Liz White Designs

Printed and bound by
L.E.G.O. SpA, Italy

This book is typeset in Venti CF, Komu and Quisas.

The paper used in this book comes from the wood pulp of sustainably managed forests.

All rights reserved.

No part of this publication may be copied, reproduced or transmitted in any form or by any means, without written permission of the publishers.

A CIP catalogue record for this book is available from the British Library.

5 4 3 2

COLLECT THEM ALL

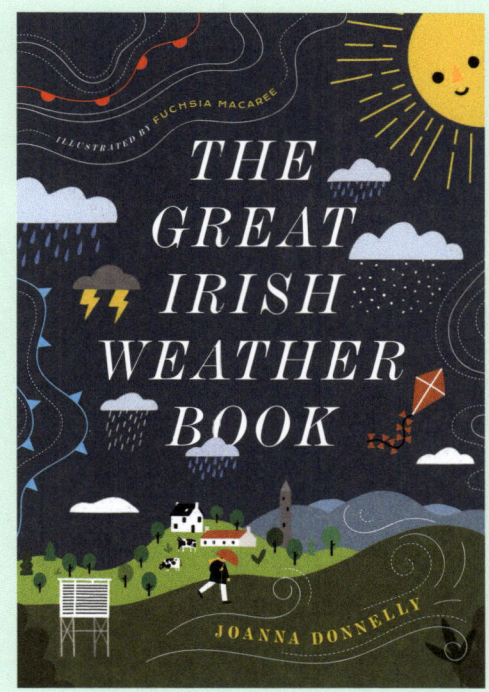
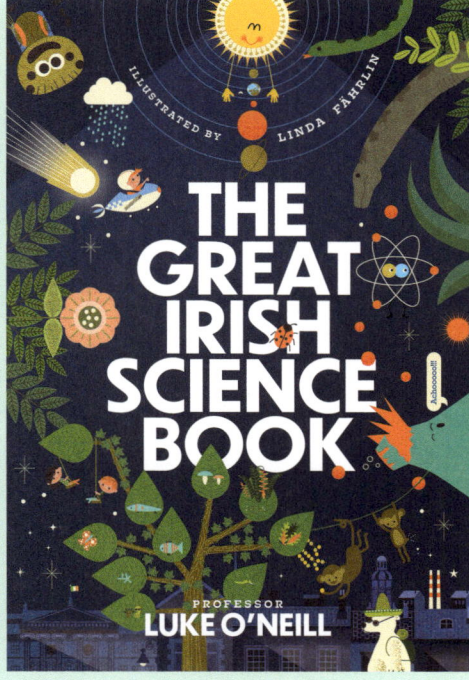
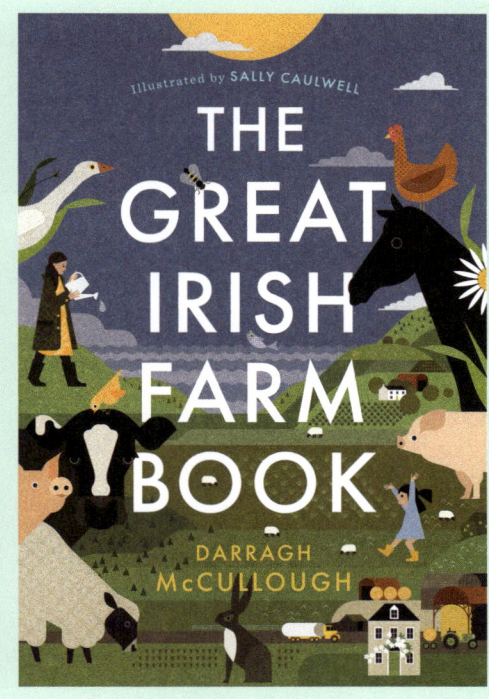

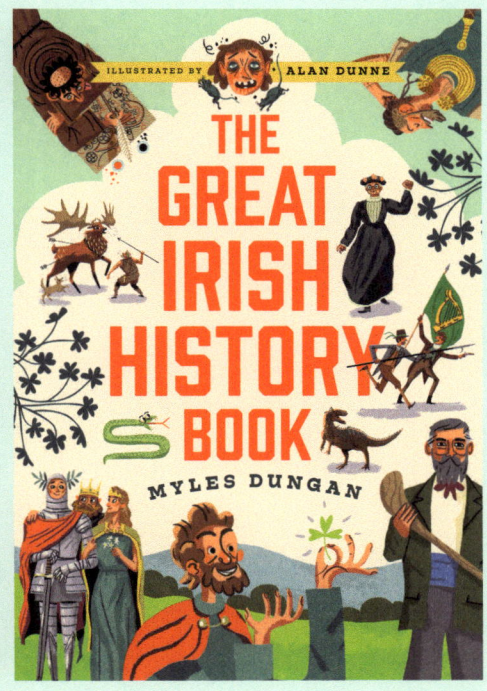